ELISABETH GILMAN

CRUSADER FOR JUSTICE

Ross Jones

SECANT PUBLISHING

Salisbury, Maryland

For information about this title, contact the publisher:

Secant Publishing
615 N. Pinehurst Ave.
Salisbury MD 21801

www.secantpublishing.com

Library of Congress Control Number: 2018931867

ISBN: 978-1-944962-53-1 (hardcover)

978-1-944962-45-6 (paperback)

Photographs of Elisabeth Gilman on the cover, and photographs and associated memorabilia of Elisabeth Gilman in the photo insert, courtesy of Special Collections, Sheridan Libraries, Johns Hopkins University

Photographs of Mercer Green Johnston and Katherine Johnston courtesy of the Library of Congress (Mercer Green Johnston Papers)

Printed in the United States of America

For Cameron, Stuart, Ross and Lynn

CONTENTS

ELISABETH GILMAN

CRUSADER FOR JUSTICE

PREFACE

She was known simply as Miss Lizzie, a name given to her in childhood by her father, Daniel Coit Gilman, and she was a fixture on Maryland's political stage for more than three decades.

By the time she died on December 17, 1950, just a few days before her 83rd birthday, Elisabeth Gilman had become one of Baltimore's best known and, for many, beloved, citizens.

An articulate and energetic advocate for social justice, she spent most of her life promoting causes aimed at improving lives of poor and ordinary citizens. No government official or agency, no leader of an industry, utility, or financial enterprise, escaped her persistent message that it was their duty to raise the quality of life for working men and women, children, minorities, and the aged.

She was respected by those who opposed her principles and she was the subject of admiration and affection of those who supported her.

Elisabeth was the youngest of Daniel Coit Gilman's two daughters. He was the first president of The Johns Hopkins University and one of the nation's foremost innovators in American university education in the late nineteenth century. She seems to have been the daughter he favored and, in her later life, she found ways to solidify his legacy as one of America's most respected academic leaders.

As a young woman in her early twenties, Elisabeth had an opportunity to attend the prestigious Bryn Mawr College, but she decided against that in favor of traveling abroad with her parents and older sister, Alice. Her diaries reveal her knowledge and appreciation of art, history, geography, culture, language, and social and political issues in the countries she visited.

She was inspired by her father's commitment to social welfare and, as a young woman, became a social worker in Baltimore. Her experiences as a social worker, or "friendly visitor" as they were called then, paved the way for her lifelong dedication to the wellbeing of the nation's workers and their families.

During World War I, she served U.S. forces in France, first, briefly, with the American Surgical Dressings Committee, and then with the YMCA, where she helped manage a canteen in a Paris hotel that provided rest and recreation services for troops on leave from the battlefield.

The year before she left Baltimore for France in 1917, Elisabeth attended a series of lectures in Boston and Sherwood Forest, Maryland, near Annapolis, where she listened to prominent members of the Socialist Party in the United States. Their messages appealed to her. Almost immediately after she returned from France in 1919 she said that she realized that she was, at heart, a Socialist and wanted to support Socialist causes. She also became an outspoken pacifist.

One of the speakers at the Sherwood Forest conference was Mercer Green Johnston, an Episcopal priest whose progressive views about social justice had resulted in him being banished from his pulpit. Elisabeth became a "disciple" of his in a somewhat strange relationship that would last for the remainder of her life.

In her early sixties, she was a candidate for political office on the Socialist ticket, running for governor of Maryland, the U.S.

Senate, mayor of Baltimore, and even sheriff of the city. She never was elected to office—the contests were never close—but she used each of her campaigns to educate the public about the fundamental principles of Socialism, as she knew them, and how those principles, if adopted by government, would benefit society.

Ask anyone in Baltimore today, "Do you know who Elisabeth Gilman was?" and the response likely will be, "Elisabeth who?" Some might associate her name with the prominent independent school for boys in North Baltimore. Some may know of Gilman Hall on the Homewood campus of Johns Hopkins University. Each of them was named for her father. Almost no one will have heard of Elisabeth Gilman.

But if they could leaf through the boxes of papers, letters, diaries, scrapbooks, newspaper clippings, photographs, and the informal memoir that Elisabeth donated to the Ferdinand Hamburger Archives of the Milton S. Eisenhower Library at Johns Hopkins, or review the papers of her friend and colleague, Mercer Johnston, in the Library of Congress, they would recognize her as a pioneer—a woman who made significant contributions to her city, state, and nation in her efforts to promote social justice and public welfare during the first half of the twentieth century.

On the following pages, I have written about her life, providing as much detail as I could find, and about some of her family and others who helped shape her character and her motivation to be of service to her fellow citizens.

I have assumed that by donating such a large volume of materials to the university archives that Elisabeth Gilman may have hoped that at some time in the future someone might attempt to tell her story. If so, it is likely that she hoped that person would be a distinguished social scientist, perhaps a professor skilled in the arts of writing, teaching, and research.

But, alas, for now, at least, she will have to settle for me, a former Johns Hopkins undergraduate who was halfway through his sophomore year when she died in 1950. A one-time journalist, I had the good fortune to spend more than four decades in the university's administrative offices, all the time becoming steeped in the fascinating place that is Johns Hopkins University. Over a period of several years I have gained enormous pleasure in handling and reading the trove of materials she entrusted to the university's archives.

She and her stalwart colleagues across the country had only limited success in being elected to public office and that happened mostly in a narrow window of time at the end of the nineteenth century and the early years of the twentieth century. However, if one considers their persistent advocacy for economic and social justice for America's working people, one quickly realizes how important their efforts were to our society today.

Meet Miss Lizzie.

CHAPTER 1

JOY—THEN SORROW

On Christmas Day, 1867, in a home adjacent to the stately buildings of Yale University in New Haven, Connecticut, a baby girl was born to Daniel Coit Gilman and Mary Ketchum Gilman. Her father, who was thirty-six, would soon become one of the nation's most respected university presidents. Her mother, then twenty-nine, would become ill and die just two years later.

The Gilmans named the baby Elisabeth, which her father quickly shortened to "Lizzie." She had a sister, Alice, who was almost three at the time. Although parents are not supposed to have favorite children, it became clear, over time, that Lizzie was the apple of her father's eye.

The two shared a zest for life, energy, creativity, and, perhaps most importantly, a commitment to men, women, and children of the country's working class.

When Elisabeth arrived in that New Haven home on Grove Street, her father was professor of physical geography at Yale's Sheffield Scientific School. A few years earlier he had played a major role in the efforts to raise funds for the school, reorganize it, revitalize it, and make it into a highly respected part of the university.

In the midst of their happy home life and Gilman's fulfilling professional career, Mary became ill. She died on October 25, 1869, in Gilman's words, "after a lingering illness, leaving two children." Although nowhere in the papers of Elisabeth or her father is there any reason stated for the illness, she had been in poor health ever since she gave birth to Elisabeth.

On September 26, 1869, five weeks before Mary died, Daniel Coit Gilman, in a clear, steady hand, recorded one of his last conversations with his wife.

These are some excerpts:

She has suffered a great deal lately and she has been dozing more than usual, but in her waking hours she has been more than usually inclined to talk about herself and the children.

She said I must tell them how dearly she loved them. "They will be a great comfort to you, Daniel; Alice will remind you of our married life and Lizzie of this long sickness."

Lizzie has been a constant delight coming into the room with her cunning little ways. "Po momma ick," she has said over and over.

Alice climbed up on the bed and sang a hymn she memorized and she was so pleased when she first heard it.

Mary said, "You must tell Lizzie … what comfort she has been to me ever since she was born. She can make me laugh and smile when no one else can."

She seems to feel that Alice will remember this illness but that Lizzie will never remember her dear mama.

She said, "I used to feel so badly about leaving the children and sometimes now it comes over me sadly, but I made up my mind some weeks ago not to be troubled and not to think too much about it."

Immediately after Mary's death in late fall 1869, Gilman

contacted his then unmarried sister, Louisa, and asked her to come and live with him and help care for his daughters. She was nearby, at the family home in Norwich, about fifty-five miles away. She came at once. Louisa would bring comfort and a firm hand, stepping up to mother the Gilman girls throughout their early childhoods.

CHAPTER 2

"A SUDDEN AND ALARMING ILLNESS"

In the spring of 1872, when she was four, Elisabeth, now firmly identified as "Lizzie" by the family, became seriously ill. Later in life she wrote that she had suffered from a form of meningitis.

It was a frightful, worrisome experience for her entire family, especially for her father.

On May 18, 1872, Gilman wrote to Andrew White, his long-time friend and fellow Yale alumnus, then president of Cornell University. He told him how devastated he was by Lizzie's illness. "All my activity is paralyzed by the sudden and alarming illness of our dear little child, four years of age, who has been the joy of our household these last sad years."

Gilman had read all he could about meningitis, even sending for material on the subject from Europe.

He leaned heavily on his sister, Louisa, to care for Lizzie during her illness. And that is what she did, spending every waking hour, for many weeks, doing whatever she could to help restore her young niece's health.

She recorded the progress of the disease and reported Lizzie's condition regularly to the rest of the family in Norwich. Elisabeth saved the notes in her files. Most are undated. Here are some excerpts:

Probably late April or May 1872:

Thursday noon. I have nothing good to report today. Lizzie is less restless than yesterday but on the other hand less bright. She lies all the time tossing a little and keeping up a little whining moan that does not seem to indicate positive pain but constant uneasiness. She hardly said anything intelligible today. Still, the doctors do not think we shall see any marked change for some days, I believe.

A few days later, on Sunday, 6 p.m. May 5th:

We are having a troubled Sunday here on account of our dear Lizzie. She had a feverish turn last night, which was not particularly alarming but today she is worse and Dr. Ives says the trouble is in her head. Of course nobody knows or says what the extent of the danger is now—but we cannot help feeling anxious.

(Dr. Ives could have been the son of Eli Ives, 1779-1861, one of the founders of Yale Medical School and one of the country's first physicians to specialize in pediatrics.)

Almost a week later, on Friday evening, May 10:

Here we are at the end of another day—not much farther on than we were last night. We have been cheered, however, by decided signs of intelligence, occasional kisses and a few words, and Dr. Ives tells of helpless cases which end in recovery. So we watch and wait.

Tuesday evening: Lizzie seems to have picked up so that today the doctor only came once. She keeps to her leaf tea for her main diet but today we are trying to vary it—a little raw beef scraped fine

and spread on a thin piece of bread and with a kind of gruel said
to be very nutritious.

Louisa told her family that the weather was turning warm and
asked them to send clothes more appropriate for warm tempera-
tures. She also told them that she was having trouble finding a
nurse who would stay with Lizzie at night.

On Tuesday morning, May 14, she wrote that Lizzie is

quiet—as well as one could hope. Indeed, we think we have seen
steady tho' slow improvement since Saturday. She sleeps very nicely
and each day shows a little more intelligence and responsiveness. At
the same time, as she grows more conscious of her weakness and
discomfort, she seems to suffer more, now in the head, now in the
neck, now in her back, now all at once.

No date:

Lizzie seems to be gaining all the time—is quite intelligent and
like herself but does not turn her head on the pillow yet. As you
can imagine there is something to do for her every minute she is
awake—but nothing much after all.

On the morning of Saturday, May 25, Louisa wrote: "We think
Lizzie has gained again, but very gradually. Yesterday I think was
the most comfortable day she has had and it was followed by a
very good night."

There is no record of further letters from Louisa but she com-
piled brief notes summarizing Elisabeth's health on certain days.

Saturday, June 22. [Lizzie] was carried downstairs for the first time.

Sunday, June 23. [With] her grandparents in the parlor.

July 6: was carried into Mr. Farnan's place.

Sunday, July 7th went for a ride for the first time. Rode every day and gained every day.

August 1st: Was taken to Norwich—just beginning to walk. Has discarded wrappers and other signs of the invalid—daily tonic of iron, quinine, strychnine.

September 20: Returned to New Haven quite well except for teeth.

Later in life, Elisabeth often commented on her health, including problems with her teeth. In letters to family, she made special efforts to assure them that she was feeling well, even robust, and was able to undertake vigorous physical activity. No doubt the months young Lizzie spent fighting the potentially fatal illness, in an age long before the advent of modern medicines, had a lifelong impact on her and her family.

CHAPTER 3

UNIVERSITY OF CALIFORNIA YEARS

In 1870, based on his distinguished reputation at Yale as a geographer and librarian, and on the success of his work at the Sheffield School, Daniel Coit Gilman was invited to become president of the recently founded University of California. He declined. But two years later the California Regents asked him again. This time he accepted. He saw it as an opportunity to lead a new university where he might be able to introduce some of his novel ideas about what an American university education should be toward the end of the nineteenth century.

Another important consideration for him was that Lizzie's doctors thought that the California climate might have a positive effect on her health.

Neither Elisabeth's papers, nor her father's, give details about the coast-to-coast move the family made to Oakland, then the home of the university. Gilman's "Autobiographical Chronology" simply says, for the year 1872, "Set forth for California with Alice and Lizzie and Aunty Lou, Dear." Lizzie took her first long train ride at age five—a trip that probably took at least five days, based on accounts of the day.

With Daniel Gilman consumed by the demanding task of leading an almost-new university, and planning for a new campus at
Berkeley, across the San Francisco Bay, it was up to Louisa to take
care of the girls. Any record of how they may have passed their
time in those days has disappeared, but one can imagine that she
took the girls on long walks so that Lizzie could exercise and be
outside in fresh, moist air coming off the Bay.

Louisa may have introduced them to games that would have
appealed to little girls in the late nineteenth century—like hop
scotch, jacks, jump rope, pick up sticks, blind man's bluff, tiddly-
winks, and hoops.

She may have taught them lady-like etiquette of the day, probably reading to them and encouraging them to read, to spell and
do simple math and art. She was their substitute mother, their
aunt, their teacher, their governess—and she showered them with
much love and affection.

Daniel Gilman knew how fortunate he was to have his two
young girls cared for by his sister Louisa. As he prepared to leave
the house in Oakland and move to the University of California's
new campus at Berkeley, he wrote to her to express his appreciation.
May 16, 1873:

One of the last acts before I surrender this house, shall be the writing
of a line to you to thank you with all my heart for your cooperation this winter. I know you did not want to come, but from the
moment when you decided to do so, you have generously & unself-
ishly entered with enthusiasm into my plans, & I feel as I have often
said that not only the children and I but the University is greatly
indebted to you for coming & helping. I think that in no six months
of their lives have our little folks been better physically & morally
than they have been, & they owe to your incessant watchfulness

& care their daily health & happiness. You don't like to have me say very much so I forebear, for if I would try to add all I think, I suppose that even California would not contain the books which I might write in your praise! Do keep yourself ready for what will turn up next and keep a sharp eye on Alice and Lizzie & believe me ever your grateful and devoted brother.

It is not clear where Louisa and the girls were at the time but they may have returned to Norwich during his move. Daniel Gilman officially opened the new Berkeley campus in September 1873, and his family was back in California at Christmas, 1874.

Though Gilman was cordially received by the university community in Oakland, he faced many problems in his new role. There were great debates among the faculty, the Regents, the Legislature, and others outside the academy about the mission of the university. What should its primary focus be? Agriculture, arts and letters, mechanical arts, science, mining, or "practical" education? Should the university be sectarian or non-sectarian? There were strong advocates for each.

Gilman was frustrated by the emotional appeals made to him to steer the university in one particular direction or another. He wrote to his Yale classmate and close friend, Andrew D. White, president of Cornell University, "I should like not to go through such a tussle again."

It is not difficult to imagine Gilman's secret joy upon receiving an invitation in late 1874 to consider becoming the founding president of The Johns Hopkins University in Baltimore.

CHAPTER 4

THE MOVE TO BALTIMORE

Baltimore industrialist Johns Hopkins died on December 24, 1873. He had left nearly all of his estate to create a university and a hospital. The bequest, consisting almost entirely of shares of Baltimore & Ohio Railroad stock, was valued at $7 million.

In the months after his death, the university trustees, all friends chosen by Johns Hopkins, consulted widely with college and university presidents to find someone who could create a new institution of higher education that would be distinctly different from the 400 or so colleges that already existed in America.

Three key consultants, all sitting presidents, were Charles W. Eliot of Harvard; James B. Angell of Michigan; and Gilman's friend, Andrew White of Cornell. Angell recalled that, "without the least conference between us three, we all wrote letters telling them (the Hopkins trustees) that the one man was Daniel C. Gilman of California."

Elisabeth remembered the excitement surrounding her father's decision to leave California for Johns Hopkins in 1875. In her informal memoir she wrote:

About Christmas time in 1874, a little girl of seven in California, whose father had gone on an important trip to Maryland, heard with interest the text of a telegram from him. It read, "Chesapeake oysters have a very fine flavor." Not comprehending its cryptic meaning, she innocently repeated it to inquiring friends and so let the cat out of the bag.

My father ... had been asked by the trustees of the new foundation created by the Will of Mr. Johns Hopkins to come east and discuss with them his ideas about the new university. Their conference was highly satisfactory and he was asked to become its first president.

The family moved from California to Baltimore early in 1875 and took up residence in the Mt. Vernon Hotel, formerly a mansion where President Abraham Lincoln had been entertained, at 702 Cathedral Street.

Daniel Gilman, the girls, and Aunty Lou were living in the hotel when Gilman was inaugurated president of Johns Hopkins University on February 22, 1876. It was a date to celebrate George Washington's birthday, the country's centennial, and the founding of a new university. It is the day the university has celebrated ever since as Commemoration Day.

Elisabeth remembered that special occasion.

A delegation of his old colleagues came from New Haven and there came also my grandmother and grandfather Ketchum, bringing along with them my little cousin, Bessie Eaton. We sat together in a proscenium box at the old Academy of Music (on Howard Street near Centre Street) taking in as much as eight-year-olds could of the speeches.

Harvard's Charles Eliot, the principal speaker, artfully linked the new university to the nation itself, and Gilman to America's first president: "We may say that the university's birth takes place today, and I do not think it mere sentiment should we dwell with interest upon its concurrence with the centennial year of our national birth, and by the birth day of him who led the nation from the throes of battle to maturity and peace."

Following Eliot's remarks, Daniel Gilman gave his inaugural address. The speech has been reprinted many times and is generally accepted as having set a course for the university, which is largely followed even today.

Elisabeth, in later life, often referred to her father as a "radical" in the world of higher education. By that she meant that he argued for, and brought, fundamental change to college education as it existed in the United States in the late nineteenth century.

Daniel Gilman was a man of big ideas and a restless innovator, seeking one path, then another, as he searched for ways to bring his progressive ideas to fruition. In his early years he had a major role in founding Yale's Sheffield Scientific School, which had an innovative program embracing both science and the liberal arts. He had hoped to introduce new ideas about advanced education and research at the University of California, but he was stymied by political battles about the mission of the university.

Finally, at Johns Hopkins, he was able to present his ideas for a new kind of higher educational institution, one which incorporated postdoctoral work and research to create new knowledge, along with more traditional teaching practices.

In England he had observed that in choosing faculty, universities sought either a gifted teacher or a good investigator. Gilman wanted Hopkins to attract faculty who had both qualities.

In his detailed examination of the early days of the university *(Pioneer: A History of the Johns Hopkins University 1874-1889),*

Hugh Hawkins said of Gilman and his colleagues, "What brought their institution immediately to the forefront in American education was their determination that the long-ignored investigative function of the university be given new stress."

Elisabeth remembered a celebration following her father's inauguration: "In the evening there was a reception at the Mt. Vernon Hotel, in which we chanced to be living that winter, and we little girls were allowed to come down for part of the festivities."

During the summer of 1876, Aunty Lou took Elisabeth, eight, and Alice, eleven, to Europe. Perhaps their absence allowed Daniel Gilman to focus fully on his new and demanding position at Johns Hopkins. Or perhaps it was just another occasion for Louisa to travel. The Gilmans were a "traveling" family.

That winter (1876-77) the Gilman family moved again, this time to a rented house on Charles Street, between Eager and Chase Streets. Elisabeth had fond recollections of that house. She recalled, "There my father had his library about him again and it was delightful to have him write out questions and to hunt for the answers in encyclopedias and other books."

While books helped to introduce Elisabeth to the world beyond Baltimore, she also was able to broaden her horizons by meeting, talking with, and listening to many famous men of that day who were guests of her father at Johns Hopkins, as lecturers or public speakers.

Two special guests that winter were Francis Childe and James Russell Lowell. Childe, an American scholar, educator, and folklorist, was professor of English at Harvard. Lowell was a literary critic, poet, Harvard professor, and later ambassador to Spain and the United Kingdom.

Lizzie seemed particularly fond of Professor Lowell. One evening, she later wrote,

Mr. Lowell led me into the dining room for supper, bending his knees so as to be almost as short as I was. I remember also that he told me the Scandinavian story of the 'White Bear.' I long cherished the books, 'Grimm's Fairy Tales' and 'Swiss Family Robinson,' which these kind friends from Harvard gave me.

By age ten, Elisabeth already had lived a very full life—having been exposed to experiences that stretched her mind, tested her emotional strength, and helped establish her personality.

In a relatively short period of time she had lost a mother she never really knew, suffered and recovered from a serious illness, and made two round-trips to California, finally settling in Baltimore. When she arrived in the city that would become her lifetime home, she quickly was caught up in the busy life of her father and she absorbed his energetic and creative style of leadership.

Another major event in her young life was about to unfold. Her father told the family he was marrying again.

CHAPTER 5

A NEW WIFE, NEW MOTHER, NEW HOME

The name of Daniel Coit Gilman's new bride was Elizabeth Dwight Woolsey. Friends and family called her Lilly.

She was descended from a long line of prominent Connecticut residents. An uncle, Theodore Dwight Woolsey, was president of Yale University from 1846 to 1871. Daniel Gilman's notes for 1877 recorded: "June 13. Married in Newport, Rhode Island, Elizabeth Woolsey and spent the summer in Europe (June 20-September 1)."

Among Elisabeth's stepmother's papers are several items relating to the wedding, including the invitation and newspaper accounts of the occasion.

The handsomely engraved invitation read: "Mrs. John Woolsey requests the pleasure of your company at the marriage of her daughter, Elizabeth Dwight Woolsey, to Daniel Gilman on Wednesday, June 13, at one o'clock. Rhode Island Avenue, Newport, R.I."

The residence was not identified by a number; everyone invited was presumed to know exactly where the Woolsey home was.

The wedding ceremony, performed by Rev. George J. Magill of Newport's Trinity Church, was one of the highlights of the wedding season that year, according to newspaper accounts.

The *Boston Globe* headlined: "A Fashionable Wedding at Newport R.I. A College President Married." The *Globe* reported that
the wedding "attracted a great deal of attention in literary circles,"
noting that the bride was the niece of Yale's president Woolsey and
daughter of the late Professor John Woolsey and sister of "Susan
Coolidge," writer of children's books.

"The Bride's family is among Newport's best treasures, beloved
by all for their kindness and loving dispositions."

A society page columnist gushed:

It was a charming wedding in a charming household. Three years
ago a trio of sisters built a house here and made a home for themselves, which any one might covet. A few days ago President Gilman
of Johns Hopkins came and took away one of the three, Miss Lilly
Woolsey. I fancy there has never been a daintier, prettier wedding
than this.

Elisabeth recalled years later: "To my sister and me the stepmother became in a very beautiful way, a real mother. Her charm,
intelligence and her graciousness as a hostess won her friends on
every side."

Not long after the Gilmans returned to Baltimore from their
European honeymoon the family moved again, this time to a town-
house formerly owned by the founder of the university, Mr. Johns
Hopkins, at 81 West Saratoga Street. The trustees of the university
had made it available to the Gilmans.

With the arrival of the new Mrs. Gilman, Aunty Lou departed
from Baltimore and returned to Norwich and, according to Elisabeth's memoir, "later married a New Yorker, Mr. George W. Lane,
who was an attorney."

(Although Elisabeth identified Lane as an attorney, New Yorkers knew him as the owner of George W. Lane & Co., a tea trading company. For many years he was president of the city's Chamber of Commerce and president of the board of trustees of Presbyterian Hospital. Interestingly, Louisa had married the former husband of her deceased sister, Harriett.)

Elisabeth remembered her family's new home on West Saratoga Street as being too large.

> When our butler, Philip, heard of the proposed move to the house, he asked permission to take the key and view the new scene of his labors. His report was "It's miles too big for us…but we must make the best of it."
>
> There were 18 steps to be kept clean, and I recall that mother feared that the daily scrubbing had not been good for the health of her 'outside' man.

Because the house was so large, a portion of the third floor, the attic, was closed off. However, one room up there "was given over to me and my friends," Elisabeth remembered. "We named it Attica."

Whenever Alice and Lizzie tired of playing outside with friends in the neighborhood, she wrote, "we could adjourn to Attica to play various games. In the spacious hall on the ground floor there was a billiard table which we thought the grown-ups enjoyed as much as we."

CHAPTER 6

A LIFELONG LEARNER

Elisabeth received much of her education at her family's home on West Saratoga Street. Her classroom, she wrote, was "the room above the dining room, with a desk and blackboard." But the room served other purposes, too.

> In off hours, it was a fine place for battledore and shuttlecock, and for declaiming our favorite verses. It was a good place for wrestling matches, too, but these were ruled out by the grandmother of my most intimate friend as unchristian, and, as religious-minded little girls, we were bowed by her decision.

For a brief period, Elisabeth was enrolled in a private school for girls, Miss Hall's School. There she learned "the three R's, long division being the hardest hurdle." When she was eleven, she suddenly was unable to see properly. It was serious enough that she could not continue at Miss Hall's. "The oculist ordered spectacles and forbade close work," she wrote.

Her father engaged a private tutor, a "Miss Wardell," who would teach her at home. Elisabeth described her as "a kindly disciplinarian but strict."

She remembered that her teacher "was of a family that had sympathized with the South during the Civil War" and that the United States history portions of her lessons were influenced by her Southern bias. That did not set well with her father "who preferred a textbook by a Northern Colonel, Thomas Wentworth Higginson" who, in civilian life, was a Unitarian minister, abolitionist, and author.

Elisabeth's eyesight problems presented a challenge for Miss Wardell. She had to "devise a special technique of study with little use of books." The teacher dictated problems in arithmetic, algebra, and geometry and Elisabeth wrote them on the blackboard, where she could read the figures and words easily.

Despite her vision challenges, Elisabeth was fond of reading and recalled "my joy when my father first gave me twenty-five dollars to spend for books of my very own. This was before the founding of the Pratt Library and I often went to the children's section of the Mercantile Library on St. Paul St. My father guided me along good lines, introducing me to Swift, Goldsmith and Hawthorne."

She also indulged in fantasy. The following manuscript, handwritten in 1881 when she was about fourteen, is among her papers. It is entitled "The Adventures of a Button," written "by two young friends" and "lovingly dedicated by the authors to Alice G."

In it, Elisabeth gives life-like qualities to buttons and takes them on different adventures. Given that she never married, the final chapter of this little story is interesting.

The first of my positive lovers was a hunchbacked old man, he
Was very rich but I did not care for him at all ....
It was a mild evening and I was sitting on the
Porch when I heard a voice in front of me saying, "How do you

Do, Mademoiselle?"
"Oh how do you do Monsieur Courie (for he was a French man),"
I replied.

"Is Mademoiselle enjoying herself in the pleasant evening air? We
Can have a nice little chat."

After running off his speech, he became awkward and sheepish,
Rubbing his hands. At last he broke out suddenly, "I came here
On very special business. I have enjoyed your company exceedingly
And I want to know if you will go to London with me and marry
Me and live with me forever?"

I may have had doubts in the beginning about accepting him
(for he was awfully rich) but his awkward way of putting
It decided me at once and I said coolly, "I thank you kindly sir
But I cannot think of accepting your offered hand." I saw
His hopes were dashed asunder and he managed to say,
"Good evening."

I had many of these offers, some even from handsome and rich
Young men but I determined to remain a maiden lady all my days.

Throughout her young life, Elisabeth's education was enhanced
by her exposure to the wide variety of academics and leading
citizens of Baltimore who had come to her home. She had fond
memories about some of her father's visitors.

   She wrote about an encounter with "Lord Bryce" (he was James
Bryce, the British politician, diplomat, and author of a three-vol-
ume book about the United States, *The American Commonwealth.*)
"I expressed a desire to study his 'Holy Roman Empire.'" Miss

Wardell allowed her to do that, "but when it became difficult, I was not allowed to drop it for something easier."

Perhaps a little miffed by her teacher's strict ways, Elisabeth wrote that she was "delighted when Lord Bryce gave me a question which he said my teacher might not be able to answer. 'What is the only French possession in 1881 within the boundaries of North America?'" Lord Bryce remained a family friend until his death in 1922.

At seventeen, Elisabeth entered Springside School in Chestnut Hill, just outside Philadelphia, Pennsylvania. Her courses there were to prepare her for entrance into the nearby Bryn Mawr College. But she never enrolled in Bryn Mawr. She opted instead for a life of travel with her parents and Alice. She got an "education" by taking extended trips to many countries in Europe and the Middle East.

Her travels abroad became her classroom. She learned about the geography and history of other countries, the social practices and economic realities facing their citizens. She had read about great art and architecture and then was able to see much of it for herself during her travels. She was devoted to music and the theater and reveled in attending performances wherever she went. She had studied French in school and, with the help of her tutors, became fluent in it as the years passed.

As she matured and as she traveled abroad almost every year, Elisabeth became an astute observer of all that she saw. Wherever she went she critiqued the architecture and art she encountered. She recorded her opinions of musical events and the people she met. Her reviews of hotels, restaurants, and life aboard ship were early versions of modern day travel "ratings."

She had an appreciation of beauty, whether in the architecture of massive, classical cathedrals or the simple scenes of a morning sunrise over the Bay of Naples. Anyone reading her travel diaries has no difficulty in grasping the scenes Elisabeth describes. Her clear, handwritten notes easily carry the reader along with her wherever she might have been traveling.

Even though Elisabeth would not formally attend college until much later in her life, she had received a broad education in her youth. The tutoring she had received, the knowledge gained at Springside School, the wide range of books she had read on the recommendation of her father, her travels abroad, and her constant exposure to her intellectually gifted parents and their friends allowed her to move with confidence and ease wherever she went. And she loved stimulating conversation, on a wide range of topics.

It was not until she reached mid-life that Elisabeth, perhaps as part of a restlessness she was feeling in 1915 and 1916, explored the possibility of formal coursework at Johns Hopkins. She was admitted as a "special student" in one of the Johns Hopkins divisions known as "The College for Teachers." The College had its roots in an idea promoted by her father in the earliest days of his presidency—that there should be a series of special courses for Baltimore City teachers.

Elisabeth was interested in the relatively new, and growing, field of psychology. At the time she enrolled, Johns Hopkins had on its faculty, and as chair of its psychology department, one of the most famous psychologists of the day, John B. Watson.

Watson, who had earned his PhD from the University of Chicago, had been a student of such well-known educators as John Dewey, James Rowland Angell, and Jacques Loeb. He had developed an objective approach to an analysis of behavior he called "behaviorism." Watson believed that his methodology would help push the field of psychology to new levels of respect in the scientific community.

He agreed to admit Elisabeth to his department. She later took

courses in other Hopkins departments. Her studies were interrupted by her service in France in World War I but she resumed
her coursework when she returned to Baltimore in 1919.

Although none of Elisabeth's papers makes mention of it, Professor Watson was at the center of a huge public scandal in Baltimore
in 1920, a year before Elisabeth would receive her degree. After it
was discovered by Watson's wife that he was having an affair with
his 21-year-old graduate student and research assistant, Rosalie
Rayner, he was dismissed in October 1920 for "public indiscretion."

One can only wonder what Elisabeth—a proper, unmarried,
Christian woman—thought about her professor's dalliances with
his student.

Elisabeth's only written comments about her experiences as
a Johns Hopkins student were that she had not intended to take
courses that would lead to a degree. She simply enjoyed the intellectual stimulation they provided, and the fact that she could study
at her own pace was a bonus.

However, one course led to another and one day the Johns Hopkins registrar discovered that Elisabeth's sampling of the curriculum
had been unusually complete, so much so that she needed only a
course in freshman English and evidence of her ability to pass the
entrance examinations to qualify for a Bachelor of Science degree.

She was able to produce documents indicating that she had
passed her entrance exams to Bryn Mawr many years earlier. She
enrolled in and passed the English course. All of that allowed her
to receive her degree from Johns Hopkins in 1921.

Among her papers in Johns Hopkins University's Ferdinand
Hamburger Jr. Archives is her diploma. It was awarded June 21,
1921, and signed by the then president of the board of trustees, pro
tem, B. Howell Griswold, Jr., and the president of the university,
Frank J. Goodnow.

CHAPTER 7

ELISABETH AND HER FATHER

It is speculative and presumptuous, based only on written materials, to make assumptions about a relationship between a father and his daughter. It is even worse to suggest that one of two daughters was the father's favorite.

But, in reviewing the papers of Elisabeth and Daniel Coit Gilman, one cannot miss the fact that so often he found ways to share his liberal social compass, his energy, and his commitment to social services, with Elisabeth, not Alice.

Whether it was in Baltimore, where he introduced Lizzie to the joys and stresses of social work, or on the docks of London's East End where he showed her the plight of poor, working-class people, she seemed to draw closer to him than did her sister.

When traveling abroad it always seemed to be Lizzie and Papa who strolled together around the cities of Europe, investigated cathedrals, climbed in the hill towns of Italy, or rode donkeys across the deserts of Egypt. Alice and Mama often stayed back at the hotel or chose to do something less strenuous.

In turn, Elisabeth demonstrated, in so many ways, how much she loved and adored her father. She also did everything she possibly could to help establish his legacy as one of America's great university leaders.

For whatever reason, and despite her own significant achievements, throughout her life, even at her death, she was identified with her father. On nearly all occasions newspaper articles about her began with "Elisabeth Gilman, daughter of Daniel C. Gilman, first president of The Johns Hopkins University..."

This may have given her some measure of creditability in her younger years, but did she tire of it as she grew older? There is nothing in her papers that indicates she was ever troubled by the constant identification with her father.

Gilman's fatherly, loving character left a mark on young Lizzie at an early age. In her memoir she was eager to present "a more intimate picture of my father."

"University presidents," she wrote, "usually go down to posterity as dignified men of affairs, with academic poise as if always on a platform in cap and gown." Her father, she wrote,

> was keenly alive to the interests of his children, not only buying books to stimulate any literary tastes they might have, but also willing to write a valentine for me to send to a little girl friend. I copy this, not for any literary merit, but to indicate his interest in my childish intimacies.

Here it is (written by her father when she was age 10):

A Valentine, 1878

I know a little maid
    Just the dearest in the land
And if everything were said

In her praise
I should go on for days and days
Talking of her pretty ways
  And all I said would stand.

She has brown sunshiny hair
  And her eyes are full of fun
And she has a dainty air
  And her voice
Makes every heart rejoice,
She's the sweetest little maid
  Beneath the sun.

Her name I will not tell
  That's a secret which is mine
Though I love it very dear
  I'll not whisper,
  No, nor lisp her
Pretty name in anybody's ear
But choose her for my darling valentine.

While remembering this example of her father's kindness, Elisabeth fails to mention the extraordinary pressures the new university president was facing precisely at the time he wrote the poem.

In 1878, the value of Baltimore and Ohio Railroad stock, which formed the basis of the Johns Hopkins' bequest, was suspect. The university had counted on receiving an 8 percent annual dividend from the stock, in cash, but it received only stock. Because of that the trustees voted not to spend more in 1878-79 than in 1877-78. Fearing a serious lack of cash flow in future years, the trustees sold

all the dividend shares, despite earlier recommendations from
Johns Hopkins that they retain all of the stock. It was an ominous
time and a preview of what would become a desperate financial
trial over the next decade.

In addition, in 1878, Gilman was fully focused on recruiting
faculty, winning some and losing others. He was trying to attract
goodwill for the university in Baltimore by establishing public
lectures and he was encouraging the creation of the country's
first academic journals in mathematics and chemistry. On top of
everything else, he constantly was fending off public criticism that
the university was too secular and devoid of religious associations.

In June 1878, Gilman awarded the first four Hopkins PhDs—in
political economy, mathematics, history and philosophy, and Greek
history and philosophy. Gilman and the faculty were creating
new departments and finding their way toward the creation of a
respectable undergraduate curriculum.

Perhaps there were dinner table conversations about all of these
things so that Elisabeth, as young as she was at the time, sensed
the enormous energy and excitement that existed at her father's
university. If so, one can understand her special admiration for
him and especially for his loving consideration of his children
during such tumultuous times.

But there was another incident, so serious and disturbing
that Gilman most likely did not discuss it within earshot of his
daughters.

It involved his brother, William, uncle to Elisabeth and Alice. In
1877 he was arrested in New York City and sent to prison for five
years for forging scrip of insurance companies worth $300,000. At
sentencing he described his crimes in detail and expressed deep
remorse about causing so many to lose significant sums of money,
including at least $75,000 from his brothers and sisters.

William Gilman had used the money he obtained under his scheme for personal gain but also to give generously to many charities in the city.

The scandal caused a sensation and was covered in newspapers across the country, some stories identifying William as the brother of the president of Johns Hopkins University.

After William served two years, and following considerable pressure from many influential constituents and William's family members, Governor Lucius Robinson pardoned him just in time for him to attend the funeral of his wife, Katherine, who had died in Norwich. Friends said the pain and mental anguish she suffered as a result of William's actions had hastened her death.

CHAPTER 8

THE GILMAN FAMILY AND TRAVEL

The Gilmans were a traveling family.

Elisabeth's father set an example for her—an example she followed for most of her life.

He had taken his first trip to Europe a year after he had graduated from Yale in 1852. He and a Yale friend, Andrew D. White, later to become president of Cornell University, were offered appointments as attachés to the American Legation in St. Petersburg. They sailed from New York to Liverpool, spending some time in London and Paris before reaching St. Petersburg in March 1854.

He was back on a "grand tour of Europe" in the summer of 1867 (Elisabeth was born in December that year). After being elected president of Johns Hopkins in 1875, with the encouragement of his trustees, he returned to Europe to seek out and recruit outstanding academicians who would become the core of the university's first faculty.

In all, between 1853 and 1908, Gilman traveled abroad ten times, on each occasion spending several weeks, or months, away from the United States. Elisabeth accompanied him on some of his trips.

She seems to have inherited her father's "travel gene." She often spoke about how much she enjoyed traveling.

Elisabeth's first foray abroad came when she was eight, in the summer of 1876, when she and Alice traveled to Europe with their Aunt Louisa. There is no detailed information about the trip, but one can imagine that Louisa was trying to give her brother time to concentrate on getting Johns Hopkins University organized without the added burden of caring for her, Alice, and Elisabeth. On the other hand, being a Gilman, she may simply have "wanted to go."

Elisabeth's next big trip came in 1883, at age fifteen, when she headed to England with Alice and her parents for a summer-long vacation there.

They sailed from New York for Liverpool on June 14 aboard the White Star Line's U.S. & Royal Mail steamer, *Britannic*.

The shipping company's publicity from that period reported that the journey took about seven-and-a-half days. The ship was a combination sail and steam vessel. The passenger list, a copy of which Elisabeth retained among her papers, indicated 184 passengers were on board.

Once landed, the family spent most of its time touring London, visiting St. Paul's Cathedral, the Guild Hall, The Royal Exchange, Tower of London, Bank of London, bridges along the Thames, several colleges of Cambridge University, and Rochester Castle.

It was on this trip that Gilman took Elisabeth to the London waterfront district where she could see, firsthand, the harsh conditions facing the men who worked on the docks and the difficult economic and social issues facing the women and children who lived in that area.

The family returned to Liverpool and departed for New York on September 15, 1883. They were among 275 passengers on the Cunard Line's RMS *Scythia*.

A Year of Travel 1889-1890

When Elisabeth was in her early twenties, she and Alice took an extended trip, lasting more than a year (1889-1890).

The sisters' travels during that momentous year took them from Italy, to Switzerland, Austria, Germany, France, Spain, Grenada, Seville, Tangiers, Gibraltar, Algiers, Bishara, Constantine, Tunis, Sicily, Palermo, Naples, the Suez Canal, Cairo and the Nile River, before winding up their travels with visits to Jerusalem, the Greek Islands, and Turkey. They were joined at times by Aunty Lou, their mother and father, and other aunts, uncles, and cousins.

Elisabeth's first entry in her diary for this yearlong trip, dated Thursday, March 21, 1889, began in Palermo, Italy. "We went to the Cathedral, which is very beautiful, were it not for the hideous modern dome stuck inappropriately on the old Gothic and Saracenic (Muslim) building."

On the afternoon of March 26, "we took the boat for Naples and the less said about the pleasure of the passage, the better. It was very noisy so we did not appreciate the beauties of Palermo, the city surrounded by mountains and sea."

They spent about a week in Naples visiting nearby towns, and then it was on to Rome where she and Alice spent another week.

They left for Bologna on May 1, stayed there for a day, saw the major tourist sights and left the next day for Venice. There Aunt Louisa had joined them. She and Alice "took Aunty Lou for her first sight of St. Mark's and the Piazzetta and we had a nice walk seeing things that we did remember having seen before."

On Sunday, May 5, "Alice and I went to the English service at Mr. Browning's big palace and were helped into his gondola by one of his sailors, so handsome! With a picturesque red sail."

"Mr. Browning" was Robert Wiedeman Barrett Browning, son of the poets Robert Browning and Elizabeth Barrett Browning. He had bought and restored a Baroque palace on the Grand Canal known as Ca' Rezzonico.

They stayed in Venice almost three weeks, where Elisabeth took Italian lessons, "lots of gondola rides, walks along the narrow streets, went over to the Lido and took afternoon tea and walked to the beach. The sun was shining and it was altogether a most satisfactory way of spending our last day in Venice." It was May 20, 1889.

In the last few days of May they were in Verona and Mantua. In June they spent five weeks "delightfully" in Bellagio, where they were joined by "aunties and cousins." Then it was off to Lucerne, Switzerland, and Innsbruck, Austria.

Perhaps Elisabeth was tiring a bit from spending so much time with her diary because after Innsbruck, she simply wrote "From there to Nuremberg via Munich." After an extended stay in Dresden, Elisabeth and Alice left and "on the 24th of October reached Paris & stayed at a pension until Mama & Papa arrived two or three days later."

Daniel Coit Gilman and Elizabeth had come to Paris to take a break from his duties at Hopkins, where he had just concluded his 12th year as president.

Earlier that year, in January 1889, Francis T. King, chairman of the Johns Hopkins Hospital Board of Trustees, told Gilman that ill health would prevent him from organizing the new hospital. He asked Gilman for his help.

On January 25, 1889, Gilman took on the added assignment of becoming the temporary director of the hospital. It was a major and critical undertaking—making appointments to the medical staff, preparing for the opening of the hospital, issuing progress reports to the trustees, holding conferences and the like.

By March he was beginning to feel the strain of leading both the university and the hospital. He requested, and received, a long vacation—from October 16, 1889, to July 7, 1890. Always finding peace and relaxation in travel, he and Lilly headed to Europe.

In early November the family visited the French seaside town of Biarritz, "arriving there late at night," and four days later they were on the train to northern Spain, heading for the city of Burgos.

On the 12th of November, wrote Elisabeth, "We took the night train to Madrid."

On November 16 "the American Minister" invited the family to dinner. He was Thomas W. Palmer, a former U.S. Senator from Michigan, who had arrived at his post in June, having been appointed by President Benjamin Harrison. Elisabeth described the dinner as "informal, the adopted baby boy, aged 32 months being at the table. He did great credit to his parents, adopted or otherwise, for he behaved with great propriety."

That evening Mr. Palmer took the family to the opera house to see Bizet's *Los Pescadores de Perlas*. They sat in a box "on the same side of the house as the Royal box. The Infanta, sister of the King, was there but we could only see her arms!"

> The house is brilliant and there are many pretty women & pretty gowns but one could hardly enjoy the music as there was so much talking on all sides. During the entre acts much smoke came into the house from the foyer & the gentlemen put on their hats in the parquet [the main floor of the opera house]. In more ways than one it was a strange contrast from the German opera, which I greatly prefer.

Elisabeth and her father "went to the market early in the morning, some of the stalls covered by umbrellas, the money changers with their pennies in front of them, great displays of yellow, blue and white Cordova pottery, nice bright colored vegetables and, fortunately, few beggars."

In Granada, Elisabeth was much impressed by The Alhambra, the 14th-century palace and fortress of Moorish monarchs. For her it was a "perfect delight" and "we went from court to court and room to room and each piece of elaborate stucco work or piece of tiling seeming more beautiful than the last."

Writing in her diary the night before leaving Grenada she said,

It is easy to give data about the buildings but the impression of beauty of the place & the wonderful skill of the Moors, I cannot pretend to give. The Spaniards drove this civilized people from among them & then showed their own barbarity in art by building a hideous palace. Why is it that people so seldom appreciate their blessings?

In December, the Gilman family stayed in Seville for 12 days, visiting the Alcazar, looking at art, and buying "some of the old Moorish tiles."

One day they visited a cigar factory.

Here there were over 600 women at work, many babies in cradles beside the tables and an overpowering odor of tobacco. The women were healthy looking and the younger ones chattering & jolly & many had a great deal of black hair and fine eyes but in my opinion there was not a great deal of beauty.

In mid-December, the Gilmans boarded *La Ville de Tangiers* for a "passage quite disagreeable of about eight hours [overnight]" across the Mediterranean to the city of Tangiers. The water in the harbor was too shallow to permit the boat to dock, so "we were taken down the side of the ship and rowed up to a little wharf."

Here her father had arranged for a guide to meet them. Elisabeth recorded in her diary

> a splendid Moor in his white turban who towered above Papa. His name was Mahomet…tall and handsome and dignified. I feel like an inferior creature here when I walk behind him. The princely figure took us up to the nice English hotel, the Continental, and is now our guide for Tangiers. We have heard that he has 140 wives, so that it may be sure that he does things in a lordly style.

Mahomet led them all about. They rode mules and followed him "into the country, on the sandy road to Fez, through some orange groves, the trees laden with fruit."

In Tangiers, Elisabeth saw "people of all shades of brown. There were also black men, slaves & servants from the Sudan & other parts of Africa. Mahomet said he could buy a slave for ten to twenty pounds."

When they visited the "Harem of the late Governor … Papa had to stay outside."

> The ladies were seated on low divans in the little room opening into the court. The one who seemed to be the chief sat apart from the others & shook hands with us…and offered us milk (goats milk!) to drink. The women were amused with any article of jewelry we had on. They took us upstairs and showed us the bedrooms. There was one real bed & other divans in one room.

The day before departing, Elisabeth wrote, "Papa and I rode out with Mahomet and had the most beautiful view of the undulating & hilly country, the sea and the coast of Spain. Later we shook hands for farewell with our handsome Mahomet." They left that night, by sailing ship, for Gibraltar.

They arrived "early in the morning & the light as we were rowed in was exquisite. The Rock does not jut out into the sea as I had supposed. The precipitous side comes down on a meadow & beyond the meadow is a bay."

On December 24, the family visited a market "where there were many Arabs selling eggs and other eatables. Spanish oranges were in great profusion but the display of fruit was not really so fine as it would be in the Lexington Market [in Baltimore]."

The following day, December 25, was Elisabeth's twenty-second birthday. The family had prepared a surprise for her.

After dinner I went into the drawing room & there found a birthday cake for me burning away its pretty slender tapers & with a red coated soldier on the top! It was so jolly...but I must confess that most of the guests were pretty solemn. That some of them feared for the future perhaps, how else can I account for the solemnity. After having been polite quite long enough, we retired to Mama's little room & had our little Xmas jollification with presents & a mysterious letter from Mahomett ben Hodge etc.!!

(Perhaps a humorous, fictitious letter, written by her father, and based on her admiration for their Arab guide?)

On Christmas Day, Elisabeth "attended the 11 a.m. Parade Service at King's Chapel which was really fine, for the old Xmas hymns rang out so lustily from the hundreds of Royal Riflemen accompanied by organ and military band." That afternoon she "took a walk with Papa."

Later that evening, "about 9:30," they learned that the ship that would take them to Algiers had arrived. Elisabeth described it as being "very large with splendid decks & nice saloons and in fact the nicest steamer that I have ever seen."

The vessel was the Orient Line's *Orizaba*, built in Barrow, England, just three years earlier. A three-decked vessel, it had been designed initially to carry cargo and passengers between England and Australia. Its 7,000-horsepower engine could reach a maximum speed of fourteen knots. She could carry 126 first-class passengers, 154 second-class, and 400 in steerage.

The three-day, two-night journey was "rough, windy and disagreeable" but Elisabeth's admiration for the *Orizaba* remained high. The ship was "very steady and rode the waves very well."

"We came into Algiers very slowly as this was the first time the captain had ever brought the *Orizaba* into this port." They were taken ashore "in small boats" and went to the Continental Hotel, "one of the best I have known." For the next few days she rested, "sitting on the balcony and the terrace" in "air soft & delicious and the view of the round blue bay, the blue hills & more distant snow peaks very beautiful."

The family remained in Algiers for about ten days, taking side trips to various sites near the city: To a village, "where people live in mud huts." To the Kasbah, "where the Sultan used to live and hanged many Christians." To a mosque. To a place where "storytellers were sitting in an open place higher on the hill relating their stories to a circle of listeners and accompanying themselves on queer instruments something like drums. They were both blind."

A group of Sudanese women in the market urged them to come in to their "booth" where they "would rub us down well. I would not have cared to trust myself to their energetic arms."

They left Algiers by train on January 10, 1890, spending a night at El Horub. Then it was on to an oasis in the "desert of Sahara," El Kantara, where they "first saw camels and afterwards several caravans."

Over the next month, the family's travels took them to Bishara, Constantine, Tunis (with "bazaars crowded with men in brilliant costumes"), and back to Italy, where they departed on February 10, at 2 a.m., on the steamer *Iberia*. They were heading for Port Said, Egypt. "We arrived in the evening. It was a strange sight to see the men running on to the ship in the light of torches," Elisabeth wrote.

"In the morning, going on deck, we found ourselves going through the Suez Canal. It is quite narrow and the Arabs run along the banks hoping for pennies to be thrown at them. About 10 a.m. we arrived at Ismailia where we landed." Ismailia is the midpoint of the Canal and was founded by Ferdinand de Lesseps in 1863. From there, the family traveled by train, for about 70 miles, to Cairo.

There, Elisabeth got her first glimpse of the Pyramids "which at this distance looked smaller than I expected." Walking about Cairo's busy streets they saw "new and most entertaining things. The veiled women, donkeys, the different dresses of different kinds of Arabs. Cairo was filled with English & American visitors…"

Two days later, the Gilman family set sail up the Nile River.

CHAPTER 9

SAILING THE NILE RIVER AND
EXPLORING EGYPT

W hen the Gilmans embarked on a three-week cruise along
the Nile in February and March of 1890, they were doing
what hundreds of other well-to-do Americans and Europeans were
doing in the late nineteenth century—visiting the Middle East and
reveling in the region's exotic sights and sounds.

They were greatly assisted by the travel company Thomas Cook
& Son which, just a few years earlier, had seen a grand opportunity
to expand its family's tour business in England to the faraway—but
magnetically attractive—land of Egypt.

Through Cook & Son's entrepreneurial and creative efforts, travel
to such an exotic place had become relatively convenient and less
expensive than in the past. Cook & Son had made it even easier
by essentially taking control of Nile transportation, including the
ships, hotels, travel agents, guides, porters, and servants. In effect,
they had "industrialized" travel in Egypt, enabling travelers to see
more in less time and at less cost.

Travelers, especially those interested in Egyptian history and
artifacts, were flocking to the country. For these and others from

the cold climates of northern Europe and the United States, a trip to Egypt and a cruise along the Nile during the winter months was an extremely attractive idea.

The Gilmans left Cairo on February 18, 1890. "About 10 a.m. we set sail up the Nile." Two hours later their boat, with "a lot of passengers on board," made a landing at a small river port "and there we mounted our donkeys," which would take them on a daylong trip among pyramids.

Elisabeth was enthralled. "We were in the midst of the civilization of the ancient empire and the whole scene as well as the ruins themselves appealed to one's imagination." Later: "We went as far as its moorings for the night."

On the 21st, "About two or three o'clock we reached Assiut (about 250 miles from Cairo). Mama, Papa and I went up into the town. We stopped first at the American Mission which has a nice building and accommodates a large number of pupils, boys and girls."

On the 24th they "arrived at Dendera early in the morning." They visited the Temple of Hathor, "the Egyptian Venus with its twenty-four columns with great heads of goddesses in the entrance hall."

The next day, February 25: "Papa and I started about a quarter past eight for the long excursion on the left bank of the river. We crossed in little sailboats and then mounted our donkeys."

They visited temples and tombs, riding up "through the desolate valley without one leaf or bit of foliage." She added, "After this long morning of sightseeing we were quite ready for luncheon which we had in the outer part of a tomb." Toward the end of the day they were too tired to travel to it but "we saw the gigantic statue of Rameses II, far larger than I supposed."

On March 3, some of the passengers chose to visit "the second cataract" of the river. Others, like the Gilmans, headed for the island of Philae. They had a choice—travel there by train or by donkey. Elisabeth chose the donkey "and enjoyed the ride very much."

"After quite a ride through the desert we came in sight of the island of Philae, looking so pretty with Pharaoh's Bed [known as The Temple of Philae]. We crossed in small boats and climbing up the bank found ourselves among the ruins."

They visited "the great temple of Isis. There was a most beautiful view of the island and the picturesque and well-preserved Pharaoh's Bed. It is more the general strangeness & beauty of the whole island and its buildings which one enjoys at Philae."

"After seeing the ruins we took the sail boats down to the Great Cataract, which is in fact the river rushing down among the granite rocks that block its course."

And here she adds,

It is not the river that is the sight but the naked Nubians who float down the rapids on logs, paddling themselves with their hands. We stood on the bank watching their feats and others were quite ready for a small baksheesh [payment of a few coins] to jump into the river without even a log to keep them afloat.

After we had had enough of this sport, and a little went a long way, these savages stood in a semicircle and Mahomet paid them and then threw a handful of coppers for which they scrambled and they gave a Hip Hip Hurray.

Later that day they had their own experience "shooting" a cataract, albeit a small one. "We took the sail boats again and shot the smaller cataract and it was most interesting to see how well the sailors managed the boats in difficult places where the rocks were everywhere and the current very swift."

Luxor and Karmak

On March 4,

> We left Assowan early in the morning and reached Luxor about dinner time. In the evening we made up a party & sailed down to Karmak and we had a most enchanting time. It is something I shall never forget and yet the grand solemnity cannot be described—the columns, the court against the sky in the moonlight.

The next day, "before breakfast," she went for "a last ramble among the wonderful ruins" of Luxor and then to Karmak. "I cantered off with the sole escort of my pretty little donkey boy but before we came home the little brother, hardly more than a baby, joined us so I was nobly protected."

Elisabeth found it difficult to leave Luxor. "I almost cried on leaving the Hall of Columns."

Writing on March 6, 1890:

"We reached Balyana about breakfast time and mounted our donkeys for our long ride across the green plain to Abydos" [about six miles away].

Abydos was one of the oldest cities of ancient Egypt and one of its most important archaeological sites. "After a ride of an hour and a half we reached the great temple of Seti I."

Elisabeth described the temple in great detail, regretting that she only had about an "hour or two" for the visit. They saw the temple of Rameses II, "a necropolis or heaps of graves of people who were anxious to be buried near the famous grave of Osiris."

They returned to their steamer. That evening, "A sand storm came up at 11 p.m. & the steamer was blown away from the mooring. Some of the passengers were on shore and had to wait before they could get on again."

Moving on, they stopped briefly at Asscont and Rhoda and then, March 8, headed for Cairo, sailing "all day without stopping." As they steamed back to Cairo they saw many more pyramids in the distance "and we had a most beautiful sunset, worthy of our last day on the Nile."

March 10:

> We landed [at Cairo] about nine thirty and came up to the New Hotel. I felt badly indeed to leave the river...I have enjoyed the trip most thoroughly for there is a wonderful interest and charm in seeing the ruins of the temples and the tombs of a mighty people, now so long dead.
>
> In many of the ruins there is a beauty of form and dignity and proportion, in others more what fills our modern idea of grace and beauty, and in all there is so much to interest one and one hardly thinks of beauty as the first thing. If this is so to me, how delightful it must be to come here well prepared, knowing the hieroglyphic language and able to read for one's self the wonderful books.

By now, Elisabeth and her family had been traveling abroad for a year. Is it any wonder that she wrote in her diary: "For some reason or other we were all too tired on this day to care to do anything."

From March 11-26, the Gilmans were in Cairo, sightseeing in the city, visiting bazaars, inspecting various collections of antiquities, seeing museums and mosques, and sailing on the Nile.

The family visited the Great Pyramid at Giza, about four miles from Cairo. "It was more enormous than I had expected," Elisabeth wrote. "At a little distance it looks exactly like the pictures but when one is just beneath it, it is overwhelming and almost took my breath away."

March 14 was sister Alice's 25th birthday. "A showery day, celebrated very quietly with flowers, which are lovely here."

The Holy Lands

On March 27th they were back on the Mediterranean, heading to the ancient port of Jaffa. "At 10 a.m. we went on board the ship of the Khedival Line. There were many Arabs and Syrians lying under thick quilts or sitting about the deck throughout the voyage," she wrote.

Three hours later they landed at Jaffa and immediately went to the Jerusalem Hotel, where they enjoyed "an excellent luncheon." The Gilmans wasted no time in Jaffa. They drove to Ramleh (Ramala today) where they spent the night at a "quite comfortable" inn. The next morning they left for Jerusalem and "passed many places mentioned in the Bible, the valley where David slew Goliath, the birthplace of St. John the Baptist, etc."

Elisabeth saw many people walking toward Jerusalem, "a most motley crowd coming from all parts of the world, Jews, Russians, pilgrims, Turks, etc. It was a curious sight for at first sight one did not know who they all were."

For most of this long journey the family sought and received the assistance of the American Consul whenever they visited a place in which a consulate was located. In Jerusalem, the Consul had an unlikely name. He was "Mr. Gillman," a different spelling and no relation. He had "secured nice rooms for us at the New Hotel."

They had hardly arrived, she wrote, when "Papa and I went out for a stroll. We went down the narrow streets to one entrance to the Harem but we were not allowed to enter, without permission." The following afternoon, "Papa and I went with Mr. Gillman and others to the Mt. of Olives on donkeys. We made a large party and were accompanied by many donkey boys."

From there Elisabeth and her father went to Bethany. "We went into the so called Tomb of Lazarus, probably an old cellar, and saw the house of Simon and that of Mary and Martha. We returned along the road of Triumphal Entry. Suddenly we had a view of the city & Temple where our Lord beheld the city and wept over it."

Most of the next day was spent at The Church of The Sepulcher in Jerusalem.

For whatever reason "Papa" seemed intent on seeing a harem. On April 1, with Elisabeth at his side, they tried again to visit a harem, "but we were denied admittance."

"In the afternoon Papa and I went to the Armenian parts of the city, much of which is on Mt. Zion." They saw "the tomb of David, in the possession of the Moslems. We were not allowed to see the tomb. After leaving here we saw a procession of Moslems with banners and guns, going to worship here."

Two days later they headed to Bethlehem, "a delightful drive of an hour and a half." They visited the Church of the Nativity. "It is a most solemn and impressive place."

When they returned to Jerusalem "we were taken by Mr. Gillman to visit the Greek Patriarch by appointment."

Visiting the Greek Patriarch

The Gilman family was ushered into the Patriarch's residence by two men "in their beautiful dresses who went before us swinging their staves on the ground in perfect time. This is done only on formal occasions." Clearly the Gilmans were special visitors.

An Archbishop accompanied them to the Patriarch. They passed "many Greek priests" on the way to the "drawing room where the Patriarch greeted us, shook hands and took us up to the raised part of the room. Here his Blessedness sat down & we were about him. He had his rosary in his hand some of the time and occasionally would move his fingers over it. He is a fine looking man & very charming in his manner. We talked through an interpreter but he made all sorts of kind speeches and some jokes."

They were served "citron & quince sweet meats, of each we were supposed to take a teaspoonful, liquors and coffee. The Patriarch rose & drank to Papa's health." In all, the Gilman's were with the Patriarch for about 45 minutes and Elisabeth described the experience as "the most oriental thing I have ever done."

Friday, April 4, 1890, was Good Friday. Elisabeth attended church services in the morning and later watched, from the hotel's rooftop, the "Moslem procession forming in the temple enclosure to visit the Moses Tomb."

Later she "walked with Consul Gillman to the wailing place of the Jews. There were many of them there. Most were old men but there were also young men, boys, little children, women by this piece of the old temple wall reading Lamentations & wailing. It was a most painful and touching sight."

"In the evening we went to the Passover in the home of a Rabbi" and later went to "the stations of the cross at the Holy Sepulcher."

The following day they traveled outside the city "and went up to the hill where... many Protestants think our Lord was crucified."

On Easter Sunday the Gilmans "went to the early service in the Chapel of Abraham, part of the Holy Sepulcher...Only about 14 were present. We went at ten to the English service. In the afternoon "we went up to the Mt. of Olives for a last visit."

The Greek Islands and Turkey

On April 8, the Gilman family departed for Tripoli aboard "The Czar, a very nice steamer of the Russian Line." They were only in Tripoli for a day. Elisabeth described it as "a little place with many gardens, some bazaars & mission house of the Presbyterians."

They sailed for the next few days, landing in Turkey on April 13. The following day, "We went out early in the morning, by train, to Ephesus," which she described as "enchanting."

After leaving the Greek Islands the family spent time in France and England. Gilman found time to visit several universities in both countries and renew friendships begun on earlier visits. They sailed from Liverpool on June 28, arriving in New York on July 4.

They immediately went to Connecticut and the family home in Norwich for a brief visit. Daniel and Lilly Gilman returned to Baltimore, leaving Elisabeth and Alice with the family in Norwich for the balance of the summer.

CHAPTER 10

TRIP TO EUROPE WITH ALICE/1900

About ten years later, in early 1900, Elisabeth and Alice—both now in their 30s—sailed for Europe once again.

Elisabeth's first letter home, to her mother and father, was written on February 16. They were at sea, aboard *Columbia*, operated by the Hamburg Amerika Liner, bound for Italy.

Elisabeth said they had had a smooth trip, so far, "tho' the racks were put out for luncheon. I haven't felt a qualm but then neither has Alice and she hasn't taken a dose of Brush, so nothing is proved yet."

(The racks kept plates, silver, and glassware on the tables during periods of rough seas. Brush, about which Elisabeth commented frequently when aboard ship, was a popular remedy for seasickness. It was manufactured by the Brush Chemical Company of New York.)

Later on this voyage Elisabeth continued to mention Brush.

Brush seems to be a splendid cure for dyspepsia. You can tell Dr. [William] Osler, for I haven't taken a dose of Nux [another popular remedy for nausea] since leaving home & yet have not had a single attack of dyspepsia or mal-de-mer. My blessings on Dr. Brush! As well as Father Neptune, for it has really been a pleasant voyage.

One wonders whether Daniel Gilman would have carried his daughter's enthusiastic message to his esteemed colleague, Dr. Osler, who, at the time, had been physician-in-chief at Johns Hopkins Hospital for a dozen years.

On February 20, Elisabeth told her parents,

You would be amused by the clockwork of my days—Bath at 8 a.m, then breakfast, steamer chair on deck with a novel, & when Alice appears about 12 we take a constitutional before luncheon, then a long nap for me in my cabin, then another walk on deck, dinner, deck, good-night. Repeat this 10 times with variations for the companion for the constitutionals & you have the voyage.

Sensitive to her father's long and successful tenure at Hopkins, and perhaps wanting to flatter him a bit, she touched on subjects that would assure him that he and the university were never far from her mind.

Writing to "My Dearest Daddy" on February 21, she said she met "a Yale graduate who said the younger alumni grudged you to the Hopkins twenty-five years ago for they wanted you for Yale. I didn't tell him how much we (!) preferred Baltimore and how superior the Hopkins is to Yale."

She added, "There is a multi-millionaire on board, a Mr. Emery from Cincinnati, but I only knew this tonight, and if he leaves tomorrow, I am afraid it would be impossible to capture a stray million or two for the J.H.U." (Emery probably was the Cincinnati industrialist who headed Emery Chemical Co, later Emery Industries.)

The next day, February 22, marked the 24th year since her father was installed as president at Johns Hopkins.

She wrote, "A last page on Thursday evening, February 22nd. We haven't forgotten the dear old Hopkins, nor the dear young Prexie. I hope Mr. Wheeler made a fine speech [at the Commemoration Day ceremonies] and that everything went well, a 'great success,' in short."

(The speaker was Benjamin Ide Wheeler, one of Gilman's successors at the University of California, where he was president from 1899 to 1919. Hopkins awarded him an Honorary Doctor of Laws degree at that Commemoration Day ceremony.)

"Since it is George Washington's birthday," she continued, "we have celebrated the immortal George from early dawn when the Star Sp. Banner was played on deck, to four listeners, till early eve when we have just had a gorgeous banquet with speeches and toasts, and illuminated ice cream."

Still on board the *Columbia* on February 24, she wrote "My Dear Mother," and said they had visited Gibraltar "about three hours ashore, but filled to the brim with pleasure." She described the gardens, the market day activities where "scrably old Moors were selling their chickens and eggs and meat."

They had visited Gibraltar on a previous trip and she wrote that the "curiosity shop was much better" than anything they had seen previously, "but we remembered the trouble of packing and repacking, and did not indulge in anything except Spanish fans."

Nervi

On March 3 they were in Nervi, Italy, a seaside town center about 12 miles northwest of Portofino in Italy's Genoa province.

Describing Nervi "as the most beautiful place to rest," she added, "we don't know a soul, for we have our own coffee in our own little salon and our dinner meal at a little table by ourselves. The views are exquisite and the walks by the sea really beautiful and our Villa Gropallo all that you could desire."

"There are about a dozen English people in this house," she wrote, "mostly stiff and exclusive and the rest are German, French & Russian, the Germans being in the large majority. Lying on the terrace, it is real amusement to watch their comings and goings."

She spent most of her days reading novels. She wrote that she had just finished "a very pretty story by Mrs. [Margaret] Oliphant and now have begun 'The Prime Minister' [Anthony Trollope]." Margaret Oliphant, a Scot, wrote historical novels, and used only "Mrs. Oliphant" to identify herself as the author.

For her parents' amusement she told a story of getting acquainted with some "small boys who suggested with great glee that we should all go to Portofino next Sunday and eat and drink—in other words a Brigande picnic and I think it would be wise for me to flee the country before I learn enough Italian to become really intimate."

Alassio

By March 18, Elisabeth and Alice had moved to Alassio and Le Grand Hotel Alassio. "A lovely part of the Riviera. There is a nice sand beach but white cliffs on the left and the right, and the hotel is right down by the water."

Nervi, she wrote,

was overflowing with Germans, quite different from Alessio, a little place but there are eighteen resident English families and for our comfort and convenience there is a library, tennis court, British stores and a very pretty little English church. We went there this morning and found it quite full of nice looking English people.

Our neighbors at table-d'hote are friendly which is a pleasant contrast to the frigidity which we met at Nervi [The Germans].

Her letter concluded with, "Don't forget to bring the phenacetin pills for there is a great deal of influenza about."

(The pills she requested were for relief of pain and fever and were widely used after the drug was introduced in 1887 until it was banned in the U.S. in 1983 because of adverse side effects, including the risk of some cancers and kidney damage.)

"With love to you both, I am your devoted daughter, Elisabeth Gilman."

Her letters and diaries do not make it clear when her mother and father were scheduled to arrive or the nature of the subsequent travels with them.

CHAPTER 11

FAMILY HERITAGE AND
ELISABETH'S CALL TO SOCIAL WORK

Elisabeth Gilman was conscious of her family heritage and proud of it. On occasion she suggested that her own liberal leanings could have come from some of her ancestors. "From whence came my interest in social reform it is not easy to say," she wrote, "but it must have been somehow in my blood."

"For example, I keep in memory one of my ancestors, the hard headed Reverend Nathaniel Ward." Ward was the 17th-century Puritan clergyman in Massachusetts who some credit with helping to establish the first code of laws in the new colony.

Writing further of Gilman heritage, Elisabeth mentioned Edward Gilman, "designated in our genealogy as the immigrant ancestor, who was one of a congregation at Hingham, England, who with the rector, placed the altar one step lower than the rest of the church."

Elisabeth was also descended from Thomas Dudley, who served several terms as governor of the Massachusetts Bay Colony. She was also a descendant of "such protesting New Englanders as W. E. Channing, father of Unitarianism, and of R.H. Dana who, as a youth, took part in the Rotten Cabbage Rebellion at Harvard in 1807," when students rioted over the poor quality of Harvard's dining hall food.

Her lineage further included abolitionist Wendell Philips, and Oliver Wendell Holmes, Jr., U.S. Supreme Court justice.

Throughout her life, Elisabeth recalled her father's commitment to social justice. She said that it began when he was only 12, in 1843, when his father took him to meet the leading social reformer of the day, Charles Loring Brace. Ten years later, in 1853, Brace and a group of like-minded friends founded The Children's Aid Society of New York. Their goal was to take children off the city streets, remove them from almshouses, and provide them with education and gainful work.

While it's difficult to say what influences young people in their choice of interests and lifelong pathways, insofar as Elisabeth was concerned, there were three formative influences.

As a young woman she was introduced to the Social Gospel movement, which was popular in the Episcopal Church and other Christian churches in the early part of the twentieth century. It was a movement, mostly in the United States, whose followers sought ways to apply the teachings of Jesus Christ to the solution of contemporary social problems.

Second, her father's devotion to social reform stimulated her and suggested a path she might follow later in life.

Finally, when she was in her early twenties, in the late 1880s, the idea of social reform, embodied in the Progressive Movement of those days, was sweeping the country. Given her nature and the exposure that she already had to social welfare work, it did not take much for Elisabeth to believe that the movement was calling her to be a participant.

Issues of poverty, violence, greed, racism, class warfare, child welfare, and women's rights were some of the topics creating robust discussion across the country, especially in cities and among the college-educated citizens of the day.

Jane Addams and Ellen Gates Starr had founded Hull House in Chicago in 1889. Organized by a group of university women, Hull House has been described as a community whose main purpose was to provide social and educational opportunities for working-class people, many of them recent immigrants, in the surrounding neighborhood.

When Elisabeth was fifteen, in the summer of 1883, she traveled to Europe with her parents and Alice. Her father introduced her to Father Charles Fuge Lowder, an Anglican priest who had established a mission church to serve those working and living along the teeming docks of East London.

The family returned to London in 1886 and Gilman took Lizzie back to East London. Before the trip she read Walter Besant's book, *All Sorts and Conditions of Men: An Impossible Story*. The fictional account is the story of two wealthy Londoners who were seeking ways to improve the lives of the East Enders. They developed a plan to build something they called A Palace of Delight at Stepney Green, which would provide local residents with educational classes in the evening, and lectures, as well as leisure and sports facilities, music, and art.

The novel inspired the Beaumont Trust to aid in the development of such an institution. Construction began on The People's Palace in 1886. The standard of teaching was developed to such an extent that by the late 1890s the University of London awarded BSc degrees there and it later became a college within the university.

Lizzie and her father "went down to see the People's Palace and Toynbee Hall, in the same section of London."

Toynbee Hall had been created in 1848 by Samuel Barnett, a Church of England curate, and his wife, Henrietta. Their vision, radical at the time, was to create a place where England's future leaders would come to live and work in the East End so they could observe the impoverished people living there and consider practical solutions to the problems they found. Today, more than 130 years later, Toynbee Hall continues its work of social service.

Back in Baltimore, and perhaps motivated by what she had seen and heard in London, Elisabeth, then in her early twenties, decided to do some social work of her own. She wrote:

> A year or so after Jane Addams had devoted herself to the people near Hull House in Chicago, three or four of us young girls began another sort of work for the boys of southwest Baltimore, the 'toughs and roughs,' they called themselves.
>
> It was under the aegis of the church, and we tried, occasionally successfully, to bring the young sons of Ishmael under religious influence. It was a very absorbing piece of work, and made us realize something of the nature of poverty—how demoralizing the standards of decent living.

Elisabeth and the other young women provided evening clubs and classes for boys and also clubs for mothers, "which I am thankful to say were not the typical mothers' meeting with a dole of charity." She wrote that she kept in touch with many of those who were among the early members of the club, often helping them to find work.

Elisabeth's father did not let his presidential duties at Johns Hopkins keep him from pursuing his own deep interest in charitable work and social reform.

In 1881, believing that Baltimore needed to do a better job of assisting the city's poor, he founded the Baltimore branch of a growing international movement called the Charity Organization

Society. It was designed to bring under one roof the many charitable efforts underway in the city that were aimed at relieving poverty, preventing crime, and improving the quality of housing.

The organization's first employee was Mary Richmond, who began as a bookkeeper. She quickly outgrew that position and today is credited with being the founder of modern social work and its emphasis on casework with families. The present-day Family and Children's Services of Central Maryland, which serves Baltimore and its five surrounding counties, traces its origin to the Charity Organization Society.

Gilman encouraged Elisabeth to become active in the Charity Organization Society as a "friendly visitor"—the early version of the modern social worker. In that role she went about the city for many years, visiting the working-class homes of families in need of assistance and counseling.

Just as her father had shown her how she might engage her natural instinct to serve Baltimore's less fortunate, Elisabeth sought ways to cast a wider net to capture others who might give their time and resources to social causes.

By 1896, she was urging Baltimoreans to get involved with the boys' clubs she had begun organizing several years earlier.

"Progress and Poverty: Boys Clubs as a Field of Work to Counteract Street Education." That was the headline for an article in the *Baltimore Sun* on January 20, 1896, in which Elisabeth told readers how they might reach out to help boys in need of assistance.

She said it had become fashionable to attempt to prevent young people from getting into trouble rather than trying to reform them after the fact. But, she asked, what about those boys, twelve to eighteen years of age,

who don't want to be educated, who glory in being 'tough' and who ask little of the world except that they be allowed to 'gang their own gait?' Our attitude toward them should surely be to supplement what is lacking in their lives, to foster that which is good....

Given then the boy with little education and still less ambition, what can we give him that will rival, in his estimation, existing amusements such as playing crap, spending money in the corner saloon or going to 'athletic clubs' where the noble art of prize fighting is exhibited.

She wrote that others have wrestled with this problem and that "in most places the boys' club is the best practicable solution."

She told the *Sun's* readers that if any among them would like to start a boys' club they would "find it easy, on some street corner, to begin an acquaintance with a dozen or twenty boys and invite them to our rooms, and after they have come to us a few times, to visit them and their mothers in their homes so that we may know their surroundings."

Elisabeth suggested that it was important for clubs to provide a variety of activities "for different tastes and methods."

She advised potential club leaders

to treat these boys as we would treat our brothers, showing them that it is the abuse, not the use, of many pleasures that we condemn; that we discourage rudeness and discourtesy, not dancing; gambling not card playing, prize fighting, not sparring, and let us give them all possible recreation that is healthy and manly.

During that same period Elisabeth created a Community Workshop for the Unemployed, which provided jobs for 100 men who made bandages and simple furniture, for which they were paid $1 for a five-hour day.

She often used the local newspapers to expose what she perceived to be social injustices. An article in the December 14, 1909,
Sun reported on her efforts to try to assist homeless persons.

"Efforts are being made," the *Sun* reported, "to have a 'Night
Bureau' open for homeless people during the winter months. All
who wish to contribute can send their contributions to Miss Elisabeth Gilman, 513 Park Avenue."

In 1914, writing in the April 8 edition of the *Sun*, she complained
about conditions at a city school.

"Upon complaint of Miss Elisabeth Gilman," the article began,
"the Board of Public Safety yesterday detailed Health Commis-
sioner Gorter and Building Inspector Stubbs to make a thorough
inspection of Public School No. 115, Merrymans Lane, west of
York Road. It is a colored school."

Elisabeth had written to the president of the Board of Public
Safety "on behalf of The Baltimore Committee on the Negro Problem, composed of many of the foremost men and women of the
city."

The school is, she said, "a fire trap; it is unsanitary and the water
supply from the fire hydrant is a menace. Either the group of buildings should be thoroughly changed or pupils should be transferred
to another building. The surroundings are detrimental to morals.
There are 227 pupils in the school."

The article reported that "the frame building has been condemned before." And previous inspections "pronounced to be in
bad condition."

Elisabeth Gilman had seen conditions in Baltimore and in
London that few of her upper-class friends would ever see. Those
experiences strengthened her resolve to do whatever she could
to help lift people out of their difficult and sometimes desperate
circumstances.

CHAPTER 12

SEARCHING FOR A NEW PATH

After their trip to Europe in 1900, the Gilmans did not travel again as a family.

When they were not traveling abroad they spent large portions of their summers in Maine, staying at their picturesque retreat, Overedge, which Gilman had built in the 1880s. It was a three-story, wood-frame, shingled home with a large porch overlooking Northeast Harbor, a gracious gathering place for family and friends.

It became a National Historic Landmark in 1965. In recent years it has been advertised for rent at rates between $21,000 and $36,000 per month. It is said to accommodate sixteen guests.

President Gilman retired from Johns Hopkins in 1901. He died on October 13, 1908, in Norwich. His wife, Elisabeth's stepmother, of whom she was so fond, died less than two years later on January 14, 1910, in Baltimore.

That year, two years after Daniel Gilman's passing, Elisabeth criticized the Johns Hopkins trustees for not acting promptly enough to create a suitable memorial to him. When the trustees of Baltimore's Country School for Boys sought her permission to name the school for her father, she readily agreed. Her motivation may have been prompted by her unhappiness with the Hopkins trustees but she also would have recalled that her father had encouraged the formation of the school in the late 1890s.

Only after she agreed to let the school be named for her father did she inform the president of the Hopkins board of trustees, R. Brent Keyser, that she had accepted the Boys School proposal. He was not happy about it. In a two-and-a-half page letter, written on university stationery and dated December 15, 1910, he explained that efforts had been made immediately after Gilman's death to raise funds for a "suitable memorial to him at Homewood." But since Homewood had not yet been developed as the new campus for Johns Hopkins, those fundraising efforts had failed.

Then Keyser told Elisabeth that he had visited with her mother shortly after Gilman's death and that he had an agreement with her that the Gilman name would not be used elsewhere without approval of the university trustees.

He concluded that while the trustees "do not agree as to the propriety of the present use of your father's name in connection with the Country School, we of course respect the wishes of yourself and your sister...The committee is therefore writing Dr. Joseph S. Ames, President of The Country School, that we withdraw all objection to the use of Mr. Gilman's name..."

(Ames was the distinguished professor of physics at Hopkins and later would become president of the university. He and his wife were Elisabeth's close friends.)

Keyser and the Hopkins trustees may have been among the first in Baltimore to recognize that Elisabeth was someone unafraid to stand up for what she believed to be a correct course of action, whether or not someone else agreed.

Aside from this dust-up, as Elisabeth passed through her forties, she recorded very little about her activities. However, from brief newspaper accounts, and comments in her memoir, it is clear that she was active in the Baltimore community and engaged in social welfare projects, with her church and with Baltimore society.

She promoted the creation of homeless shelters in the city, supported the Women's Club of Baltimore, urged the federal government to protest "the forcible deportation [by Germany] of the Belgian nation to forced labor."

She frequently gave dinner parties for local debutantes. Here is a typical notice that appeared on the society page of the *Baltimore Sun* on October 29, 1914: "Miss Elisabeth Gilman has issued invitations for a dinner to be given at her residence 513 Park Avenue, in honor of Miss Evelyn Barton Randall, the debutante daughter of Bernhard Randall, on Tuesday, November 10."

During these years she remained in close touch with Alice and frequently visited her at her New York home as well as at her summer home in New Hamburg, New York. She also remained close to her father's family in Norwich and kept in touch with her favorite Aunty Lou.

She wrote, at one point, that after the death of her parents she tried to carry on the dinners, parties, receptions, and charitable events in which her parents had participated for so many years. Their home had always been a gathering place for Baltimore's intellectual and community leaders. And Elisabeth wanted to continue that, perhaps as a way to memorialize them.

But it was a life of contradiction and one that no longer appealed to her.

As she approached the age of fifty, she suddenly seemed open to the possibility of throwing off her perceived obligation to follow her parents' social commitments and to embark on a new course, something fresh and different, something that would have its roots in her experience and commitment to social welfare, and something she could call her own.

She was reaching out, searching for a new way to apply her interests and her talents to a cause to which she could bring all of her energy and intellect.

She was moving slowly but surely toward becoming one of the leaders in the American Socialist Party.

CHAPTER 13

RELIGIOUS INFLUENCES

E lisabeth's own musings about the factors in her life that led her
to embrace Socialism suggest that she was most influenced by
her father's interest in social justice. But it is also clear that, starting
at an early age, she experienced a religious calling.

She had been an active participant in the community outreach
work of her Protestant Episcopal Church, Old St. Paul's in Baltimore. Later she would associate with Episcopal clergy who were at
the forefront of a movement, primarily among Christian churches,
to apply the teachings of the New Testament to address a variety
of social issues. It was known as the Social Gospel Movement.

Once, when she was asked how she became a Socialist, she
replied: "My inspiration for Socialism is religious and I felt it was
a living sacrifice for me to make, and therefore my deepest interest
is that the Gospel of Christ should be socialized."

When the Gilman family moved to the former Johns Hopkins
mansion at 81 West Saratoga Street, after Daniel and Elizabeth
married in 1877, they were living immediately next door to the
rectory of St. Paul's Episcopal Church, known locally as Old St.
Paul's.

The rector at the time was Rev. Dr. J.S.B. Hodges (the initials

standing for Johannes Sebastian Bach). An 1850 graduate of
Columbia College in New York, he continued his education at
the Episcopal Church's General Theological Seminary, also in
New York. He came to St. Paul's in 1870 and remained rector
there for 35 years.

Hodges created the St. Paul's Choir for men and boys in 1873.
He recruited the choir boys from St. Paul's School, which had been
established at Old St. Paul's Church in 1849.

In 1888, Reverend Hodges arranged for his church to purchase
a house at 8 E. Franklin Street as a residence for the school and
choir boys. The church purchased 10 E. Franklin, for the same
purpose, in 1896.

Elisabeth must have been just as fascinated as the local residents
were by the sight of the choir boys marching along Charles Street,
making their way from the Franklin Street residences to Old St.
Paul's Church. The almost daily parade of these young men was
a Baltimore tradition for many years.

In his "A history of the first 100 years of the Boys' School of St.
Paul's Parish," The Reverend Arthur B. Kinsolving, successor to
Dr. Hodges, wrote:

> Witnesses of another era will never forget the traditional marching,
> winter and summer, of the St. Paul's Choir boys down Charles Street
> to the church in their choral robes and caps. They would proceed
> two abreast, each pair of boys marching to size, with the smaller
> ones in the front ranks.

Elisabeth was among those who cared about the boys' wellbeing, and she took a particular interest in Robert and Page Nelson,
sons of the Episcopal rector in Halifax County, Virginia, whom
she greatly admired. Wrote Reverend Kinsolving:

Robert, a very tall boy, was asked at the close of his last year at the School to make his home at her house and be a sort of protector. His youngest brother, Spotswood Page Nelson, accepted a similar invitation.

Largely through her interest and friendship, both of these young fellows were enabled to attend Johns Hopkins University and both have achieved positions of prominence in the financial world, Robert as the vice president of a Cincinnati trust company and Page as the president of the Savings Bank of Baltimore.

Elisabeth and the Episcopal Church

It is likely that neither little Lizzie nor Dr. Hodges could have imagined that the seeds of friendship that were sown nearly a half century earlier, when they lived next door to each other on Saratoga Street, would have led to Elisabeth's deep and life-long commitment to the church and its programs. It all began because she simply liked Hodges and his family.

Recalling those days in her memoir, she wrote: "He used to make me feel absolutely at home when I crossed over to play with his children. He would have been surprised to know that I kept for so many years the verses he sent me when I was quarantined by illness and which began with the stanza:

Dear Lizzy
Not being busy
I write you a letter
To say I'm glad you're better
And getting over the whooping cough.

Elisabeth described Hodges as an "Anglo-Catholic of the type of Pusey," referring to the English clergyman Edward Bouverie

Pusey, an advocate of "high church" practices in the Church of England.

Elisabeth's Confirmation took place at St. Paul's Church. In a handwritten note, among her papers, she wrote:

> I was confirmed Wed. March 24, 1880.
>
> What the Bishop said: That we all are coming forward to the site of Confirmation with very happy and glad hearts and though the benefits were very great, the responsibilities were just as great. He advised us to be at least part of each day, alone, to be alone with God. Then I think he spoke of the necessity of reading our Bibles regularly and saying our prayers. He told us how we must visit & help the poor & about coming to church.
>
> I am going to try, with God's help, to be less selfish, not trying to have my own way in everything. And to be sweeter to Alice and not be rude or saucy to Mama and Papa. Lizzie Gilman

Elisabeth wrote in her memoir: "My father, though of a more liberal faith, was glad to have me happy in this new, devout atmosphere. I throve on it, yet I was not growing up without certain influences that made for modern ideas."

Elisabeth could not have known at the time that her father, remembering his sister Louisa's devotion to her little Lizzie, wrote to Louisa to tell her about Elisabeth's confirmation. In a letter dated March 24, 1880, written in Baltimore, he sent this heartfelt message to Louisa, one that must have touched her deeply.

> We should all have enjoyed having you with us today when our Lizzie (not much longer to be called 'little') confirmed the engagement made for her long ago. Have you happened to think that she is just at the age of Alice when she came forward and that both

of them were twelve years old, the very age at which their Maker declared that he must be about his Father's business. You would be pleased if you could see the seed which you planted—Lizzie's heart is steadily maturing & how sweet & naturally without any urging from others she desires to be a full participant—all the promises. She has had gentle teaching these last three winters from her most devoted mother—teaching quite in accord with what you used to give.

Dr. Hodges of St. Paul's Church is direct & considerate & left 'the instruction' which the rules require, almost exclusively to motherly lips so I don't think Lizzie has any very sharp idea of ecclesiastical differences, but thinks that the outside variances are quite secondary & in reality she is now at one with you and me & her grandparents & Alice, quite as much as with those to whose form of worship she is now conforming.

Elisabeth remembered her father discussing evolution and the Bible. "Not only did I hear my father talk on such subjects, but we had a constant stream of distinguished visitors to whose talk we children listened."

She recalled the astronomer, Professor Simon Newcomb, Cornell University's president, and her father's friend, Andrew White, and Harvard's Charles William Eliot, among others.

She remembered a special occasion when she met the liberal English clergyman and author, Frederic W. Farrar, Canon, and later Archdeacon, of Westminster Cathedral. He had come to Johns Hopkins at her father's invitation, to present a lecture.

At the time, Daniel Coit Gilman was being criticized by some in the community for shaping the new university to be a secular institution rather than one, like so many in that time, that would have a denominational affiliation. Whenever he could, Gilman found ways to invite distinguished members of the clergy to speak at Hopkins. He invited the community to hear them. Perhaps, in this way, he aimed to assuage their concerns.

Elisabeth, probably unaware of her father's motivation in bringing Canon Farrar to the campus, remembered Farrar's remarks and wrote in her memoir, "At a lecture of Canon Farrar's I was introduced to Browning's 'Saul' and 'A Death in the Desert,' and these poems gave me the liberal point of view more effectively than any formal treatise could have done."

Elisabeth had attached herself to a church that, since its earliest days in 17th-century Maryland, had paid attention to issues of human welfare. In the mid-nineteenth century, outreach programs sought to aid the poor, freed slaves, and immigrants. And later, by the 1880s, there were numerous examples of charitable acts, organizations, and institutions flowing from the Episcopal Church.

An example is The Guild House Association, founded by Dr. Hodges. Its mission stated: "The object of our Association is to provide for our neighborhood religious teaching and services by steady, daily work for and with the peoples of Southwest Baltimore." It was an independent group but all of its volunteers were members of St. Paul's Church.

Later on, in a booklet about the Association, Elisabeth was listed as one of eleven directors. It was a broad-based social welfare agency and operated out of a building at 539 Columbia Avenue at the corner of South Greene Street.

The Guild House had a wide range of programs. Guild House volunteers mounted art exhibitions, lectured on tuberculosis, worked to prevent the opening of saloons, gave physical examinations to children, held picnics, and visited families in their homes. It was reported that, "at least 500 people come to the Guild House every week."

There was a Sunday School with more than 60 children enrolled, and an "industrial school" on Saturday mornings to teach "little girls" how to sew, which some 165 attended. There was also a 150-member St. Paul's Brigade for boys twelve years old and up (with a waiting list of 400). Gym classes and baseball and basketball games were held "under a professional instructor."

The Girls Club, with 65 members, meeting on Tuesday evenings, offered classes in embroidery, athletics and reading.

There was also a social club, a leatherwork club, a mothers' club, and a homemakers club, which met every two weeks to discuss questions of education for children "and the age at which they should go to work."

Elisabeth supported the Guild House with her time and money. For many years she and her mother and father were listed in Guild House publications as being "supporters" or "contributing associates."

As impressive as the church's efforts in social welfare might seem, the magnitude of the effort was not as large as it might have been nor were the goals of groups like the Guild House Association shared by everyone—parishioners or clergy.

In a paper, "The Anglican, Episcopal and Diocesan Heritage in Maryland," D. Randall Beirne wrote:

The Progressive Movement of the 1890s for urban reforms in politics, health, child labor and working conditions, civil liberties and welfare was dominated by Baltimore's leaders, half of whom were Episcopalians. In spite of Bishop (William) Paret's progressive views and social consciousness and the strong showing by so many in the church, a far larger number of Episcopalians were apathetic towards rapid social change.

Although Beirne found that, "Overall, the movement did

succeed in improving health conditions, working conditions and suffrage," he returned to the theme of apathy when commenting on the church's role in helping needy Maryland citizens in the Great Depression of the 1930s.

Beirne credits some Episcopal clergy for working "with other protestant churches toward improving the unemployment relief programs in Baltimore," but he adds that in spite of the efforts of a few, Baltimore Protestantism in 1935, when compared to the welfare efforts of the Catholic and Jewish congregations, was criticized by the city for "an entirely inadequate contribution to the solution of the social problems of the city. The Protestant churches and social work were lamentably far apart."

Even earlier Elisabeth had expressed her disappointment in her church's overall lack of commitment to matters of social welfare and justice.

Writing from her Park Avenue home on February 10, 1920, to the Episcopal Bishop of Maryland, John Gardner Murray, she said, among other things,

I wish I could feel that your idea and mine of Christianizing the social order were not so far apart as when we talked about such things in 1916.

I have come back from my two years over-seas, keen to go on working for the Kingdom of God on earth, but to my deep sorrow, I feel that most of the fearless leaders in this cause, are without the bounds of the Church, not within it.

You remember perhaps an ecclesiastical humorist once said, "What the Episcopal Church needs is not a Quiet Day, but an earthquake." Who knows how near that earthquake may be? The Greek Church is a dead letter, if not a dead body, as regards the mass of Russian people, and it is feared that our own Church has the barest possible influence with that great body of our American people. Yours very truly, Elisabeth Gilman.

Despite her feelings that her Church had fallen seriously short in the social reform movement, Elisabeth remained, for the rest of her life, a loyal Episcopalian and a regular attendant at services, whether at home or abroad. Perhaps her church's tepid response to social issues spurred her to try to do more, personally, for men, women, and children who were struggling to improve their lives.

Whether it was deliberate on her part, or merely coincidence, Elisabeth found clergymen in the Episcopal Church who shared her liberal views. They embraced the Social Gospel Movement and they had the courage to speak about it, publicly and forcefully.

One such person whom she met at a Socialist Conference in 1916 was the Episcopal priest, Mercer Green Johnston. He became a colleague and a nearly life-long friend.

CHAPTER 14

MOVING TOWARD SOCIALISM

I n the summer of 1916, as she neared fifty, Elisabeth's life took a dramatic turn.

That summer she met a group of men and women who shared her commitment to social welfare and justice. Most lived well beyond the boundaries of Baltimore. They were exceedingly articulate, energetic, and creative in expressing their positions and ideals.

Given her rich experience and her own mission of promoting the advancement of the Social Gospel, she had found a group of individuals who saw the world as she did.

Nowhere in her memoir or other papers does Elisabeth indicate some sort of "Eureka" moment when she suddenly felt drawn to these progressive men and women. But certainly her exposure to their strongly held opinions had stimulated her to think about the possibility of working to advance the cause of Socialism.

Encountering Vida Dutton Scudder

Those people and their ideas came into sharp focus when she attended a conference or "church institute" near Boston that summer. This is how she described the experience in her memoir:

I little thought when I went north in the summer of 1916 that I should receive a challenge to a different type of work. It came about in an odd sort of way. I went to a church institute near Boston where Miss Vida Scudder of Wellesley College gave three lectures from the Socialist point of view. I was interested but it didn't grip me.

Vida Dutton Scudder was the daughter of a missionary to India and was born there in 1861. Her father died shortly afterward and she returned with her mother to their home in Boston. She spent much of her youth traveling with her mother in Europe. She graduated from Smith College in 1884 and later studied at Oxford, where her social awareness became more acute.

Scudder was an English professor at Wellesley College from 1887 to 1927. She was a pioneer in the Settlement House movement of the late nineteenth century and, from 1893 to 1913, was the primary administrator of one of those houses, Denison House, in the rundown South Cove area of Boston. In 1911, she co-founded the Episcopal Church Socialist League and joined the Socialist Party.

Among Elisabeth's papers there is no record of what Scudder may have said at the church institute, but it is likely that her message was similar to that contained in a long paper—Scudder called it a "little book"—that was produced by Project Canterbury, a publishing project of the Episcopal Church.

Her paper was titled "The Church and the Hour—Reflection of a Socialist Churchwoman" (published by E. P. Dutton, New York, 1917).

Throughout, it is a plea for the church's leadership and its members not only to understand the needs of people beyond the church door but to do something about meeting those needs.

Scudder believed that a statement from the Lambeth Conference of 1908 supported her pleas for a more activist church (The

Conference is a periodic gathering in England of the bishops of the Anglican Church). Scudder said until that conference the Church's "expression of social faith" was limited, but that among "English speaking Christians, the first striking group-utterance of the century [about social justice] was perhaps of the Lambeth Conference of 1908."

Quoting from a report of the conference, she wrote:

> What is now needed, is groups of Christian men and women, in every place, determined to make it their aim to bring the sense of justice and righteousness, which is common to Christianity and Democracy, to bear upon the matters of every-day life in trade, in society and wherever their influence extends, and to stir up public opinion on behalf of the removal of wrong wherever it may be found, thus making an earnest endeavor to share in the transforming work of Christianity for their brethren and companions' sake.

These were the principles followed by those who worked to advance the Social Gospel in America early in the twentieth century. Vida Scudder would champion the movement. And, later, so would Elisabeth.

Even though Elisabeth wrote years later that Scudder's lectures did not "grip" her, they must have helped prime her for what was to follow.

Shortly after Elisabeth returned home from Boston, she had an opportunity to attend a week-long international conference where she could listen to speeches by the leading Socialists of the day.

She did not have to travel far from Baltimore to get there.

Sherwood Forest
As summer gave way to fall in 1916, Sherwood Forest, Maryland, seemed a most unlikely place to hold a conference of some of the

most influential leaders of the Socialist movement in the United States and abroad.

Heavily wooded on 400 acres along the Severn River near Annapolis, this bucolic and peaceful place stood in stark contrast to the crowded streets, sweatshops, and factories of America's large cities, the places where Socialists were seeking to advance their cause. Sherwood Forest was a recently developed summer retreat for wealthy residents of Baltimore and Washington, D.C.

Even the *Baltimore Sun* questioned the choice of the site. In a long editorial generally expressing pleasure that the conference would be held in Maryland, the *Sun* opined on September 21, "Sherwood Forest is a delightful spot for a conference on nearly any subject but we wish this one could have been held in Baltimore where the general public could more easily have enjoyed the educational benefit of the discussions."

And, one might add, where social justice issues under discussion were more immediately at hand.

The host for the conference was William F. Cochran, who had developed Sherwood Forest just a few years earlier. A Baltimorean, he was a curious combination of capitalist land developer and liberal socialist.

The *Baltimore Sun* said Cochran was among "a number of Episcopalians and others interested in social work and of socialist tendencies."

Cochran also had a knack for getting *Sun* reporters to write about his development projects. It was most likely that it was through his efforts that the *Sun* gave daily coverage to the weeklong gathering.

The meeting, which attracted about 200 participants (including 45 representatives of colleges and universities), was sponsored by the Intercollegiate Socialist Society, founded in 1909 by the popular novelist Upton Sinclair. Its purpose was to promote socialist causes by organizing college and university students on campuses across the country.

Exactly how Elisabeth received her invitation to attend the conference is not clear but it could have come through Rev. Richard W. Hogue, an Episcopal clergyman Elisabeth knew.

A few months earlier, Hogue, the Rector of Baltimore's Church of the Ascension, had been forced to leave his parish. The conservative members of his church had objected to his promotion of the Social Gospel.

The *Baltimore Sun*, in its initial account of the meeting on September 13, 1916, said attendees would include "economists, sociologists, socialists, clergymen and others. Of foreign representatives, Henry La Fontaine, Senator of Belgium, will be the most prominent. Senator La Fontaine, who is a Socialist, has won the Nobel Peace Prize." (The Nobel, awarded in 1913, recognized his years of work as president of the International Peace Bureau.)

Jacob H. Hollander, the distinguished professor of political economy at Johns Hopkins, represented his university at the conference. A year later his book, *The Abolition of Poverty*, was published.

Some others the *Sun* reported as being in attendance were: James P. Warbass, president of the Co-operative League of America; Dr. Helen L. Summer of the Federated Child Labor Bureau; William H. Johnston, president of the International Association of Machinists; Arthur E. Holder, representing the American Federation of Labor; and George Creel, "whose work for reform along social and political lines has caused much concern among conservatives."

Others included Meyer London, a Socialist Congressman, representing New York City's Lower East Side; Benjamin C. Marsh, secretary of the League for Municipal Ownership and Operation of New York City; and Algernon Lee, a founding member of the Socialist Party of America.

On September 19, the *Sun* published a long article about one of the major participants, Rev. Mercer G. Johnston. He was someone who, for many years to come, would have an extremely close relationship with Elisabeth.

The *Sun* headline summed it up: "Will Join Socialists—Mercer G. Johnston, Militant Clergyman, Due at Sherwood Forest Today. Plans to Work Here. Expects to cooperate with Rev. Dr. Hogue in the Field of Social Service."

Johnston, the *Sun* reported, "whose resignation from the fashionable Trinity Protestant Episcopal Church of Newark, N.J., was accompanied by a denunciation of his parishioners, will pass through Baltimore this afternoon."

In his final sermon in Newark, the *Sun* wrote, Johnston called members of his congregation "old skins" and said they were "dead as Lazarus." He also accused his Bishop, Edward S. Lines, of "entering into a covenant to force him from the church."

From the moment she met Mercer Green Johnston, Elisabeth was smitten—smitten by his confident personality, his rhetoric, his unflagging commitment to advance the cause of the Social Gospel, his courage and determination in the face of obstacles and, later, his bravery in battle. Early in their relationship, despite the fact that she knew he was married, she may have misinterpreted his expressions of affection toward her.

About a month after she met Johnston at Sherwood Forest, Elisabeth wrote (October 16, 1916): "Your friendship means so much to me and I love to think it is God given in a special way, for it certainly did come mysteriously." In the years ahead she found many ways to assist Johnston in his commitment to work for social justice in America.

Although she often addressed her letters to Johnston and his wife, Katherine, the content of those letters clearly was directed to Mercer.

The Conference

In her memoir, Elisabeth had this to say about the Sherwood Forest Conference: "I met and listened to such men as Dr. Walter Rauschenbusch, John Spargo, Harry Laidler, and Mercer Johnston." These men were among the leaders of the socialist movement in America in 1916.

Rauschenbusch, a handsome, mustached and goateed Baptist minister, at that time, was the acknowledged theological leader of the Social Gospel movement in the nation. His writings, sermons, and speeches described the commitment by liberal Protestant churches to improve industrialized society through the application of religious principles of charity and justice.

Spargo, a British-born former stonecutter, had come to the United States in 1901 to begin a lecture tour of the country in which he tried to convince Americans to follow the principles of socialism. He was a founder of the Socialist Party of America. In 1905 he helped establish the Intercollegiate Socialist Society that was host for the Sherwood Forest conference.

Laidler was a writer, a magazine editor, and politician. He later became executive director of the League for Industrial Democracy, which was the successor organization to the Intercollegiate Socialist Society. In New York State he would become the Socialist candidate for Governor in 1936 and U.S. Senator in 1938. He managed Socialist Presidential Candidate Norman Thomas's campaigns in 1928 and 1932.

The presenters spoke on a wide range of subjects.

Under the topic "Social Preparedness: National and International," the conference participants debated how to deal with social issues that would arise following the Great War in Europe, which had begun two years earlier, in 1914.

There were discussions of how to achieve peace in the world, how to address immigration after the war, and the impact of the Adamson Act, which had recently established the eight-hour work-day for railroad workers. "Consumers Cooperation" was another topic, as was "The Social Aspect of the Life of Christ."

Elisabeth listened to presentations from each of these men, and others, and she was moved by their messages. She wrote in her memoir: "I could not ignore their plea for social justice. I decided that although I was not prepared to join the Socialist Party, I was by conviction a Socialist."

A few months later, on January 2, 1917, she wrote to the New York millionaire Socialist writer and philanthropist, James Graham Phelps Stokes, to solicit him for money to enable Episcopal cler-gymen to leave their parishes and practice the Social Gospel in their wider communities.

It is likely that she was motivated to seek such support because of her newfound admiration for Mercer Johnston and her long friendship with Rev. Hogue, each of whom had been banished from their churches because of their progressive views. Recognizing they no longer had pulpits from which to speak, she hoped they might travel about the country to spread the message of the Social Gospel. But they would need financial support to accomplish that.

Whatever her purpose may have been, Stokes declined her request.

Elisabeth reached out again, this time to another prominent American Socialist, Charles Edward Russell of Brooklyn, New York. Russell was a muckraking journalist and author whose articles and books on social reform were compared with those of Lincoln

Steffens, Jack London, and Upton Sinclair.

Writing to Russell on March 14, 1917, Elisabeth sought his assistance in helping to convince Baltimoreans that Socialists are loyal Americans.

She began her "Dear Sir" letter: "Feeling that we have much in common as patriotic Americans and as Socialists, I take the liberty of writing to you on a subject that has been much on my mind during the last few days."

And here she invoked her father's name and position as she had done on so many occasions, and would do in the future, as a way to give her special standing among individuals who may not know her.

"As I am not known to you, will you let me introduce myself as the daughter of the late Daniel C. Gilman, president of The Johns Hopkins University—this in order that you may realize that I am not working in any casual or careless spirit."

She told him that there had been a negative outcry in Baltimore over the fact that several schoolchildren from Socialist families had refused to salute the flag in their classrooms. There was, she said, "the disapproval of the community against the lack of patriotism of Socialists at this very critical period in our country's history."

"Most Socialists that I know here in Baltimore are Pacifists," she wrote, "but I cannot but feel that there may be, nay there must be, a large number of Socialists who are loyal Americans."

"Next Sunday is Flag Day in Baltimore," she noted, "and it seems more than I can bear to feel that its message will be heard only by more or less conservative people...when at least a working minority of our comrades in Socialism might be willing also to honor the symbol of our country's freedom."

She urged him to think of ways to convince the public at large that Socialists can be patriots. She suggested he write such a message to Baltimore newspapers, adding that she cannot do that effectively because "I am not a member of the Party nor have I been a Socialist for a very long period. This of course makes any personal action on my part more difficult."

There is no record of a response from Mr. Russell.

Entering World War I

About six months after the conference at Sherwood Forest, the United States entered the Great War in Europe, on April 6, 1917.

Many Socialists were pacifists and conscientious objectors but Elisabeth, at that time, was not. Nor was her new friend, Mercer Johnston.

There seems little doubt that Johnston, who was eager to go "over there," encouraged Elisabeth to leave her home in Baltimore and her socialist inclinations, at least temporarily, and follow him and his wife, Katherine, to France where they would spend the next two years providing aid to American servicemen through their work with the YMCA.

There also seems little doubt that Elisabeth was eager to toss aside the routines of her life and follow this creative, energetic proponent of the Social Gospel.

CHAPTER 15

WOMEN IN WORLD WAR I

Almost immediately after President Wilson asked for a Declaration of War on April 6, 1917, buoyant young men and women, in a national explosion of patriotism, flocked to apply for military or civilian service in support of the war effort.

Just a month later the YMCA began welcoming and processing applications from women wanting to volunteer for service in France. In June, Mrs. Vincent Astor opened a canteen in the port of Brest for U.S. sailors, and Mrs. Theodore Roosevelt, Jr., organized the first canteen in Paris. Her husband (the eldest son of President Theodore Roosevelt), a lieutenant colonel, commanded the First Battalion, 21st Infantry, First Division of the American Expeditionary Forces.

The suddenness with which Elisabeth decided to go to France in mid-summer 1917 made it likely that she had no idea of what lay ahead of her.

Although most of her time in France was spent as a YMCA volunteer, she began her service with another organization.

She and her new friend, Katherine Johnston, Mercer Johnston's wife, had applied for and received appointments to serve in a workshop of the National Surgical Dressings Committee in Paris, making bandages for wounded servicemen.

Mercer Johnston had gone to Paris to volunteer with the American Ambulance Field Service.

Elisabeth and Katherine shared an apartment in Paris. Elisabeth had hoped that arrangement would allow her to see Johnston when he was on leave from his driving duties.

She could not have known that both she and the Johnstons would soon leave their initial posts to work with the YMCA—Elisabeth and Katherine at canteens, mainly in Paris, and Johnston as a YMCA secretary with the troops at the front.

One wonders whether Elisabeth would have acted so quickly to "sign up" if she had understood, in advance, that national policies regarding women who volunteered for service in France were supposed to confine their duties to those of stereotypical roles at home in peacetime—providers of good food, clean homes, and entertainment.

Most of all she could not have realized then, or perhaps even during her stay in France, that she was but a tiny part of a much larger effort, under the auspices of the American Expeditionary Forces, to recruit women to support the troops in France.

Eventually, there would be more than 16,000 women working directly for the army or, like Elisabeth, as employees of official welfare agencies working with the army. Most served as nurses, canteen workers, and telephone operators (nicknamed, affectionately "The Hello Girls"). There were about 3,200 YMCA workers, 2,500 working with the American Red Cross, 260 with the YWCA, 104 from the Salvation Army, and 76 from the Jewish Welfare Board.

Almost without exception the women were native-born and white, with an average age of almost thirty-three. Many were single and living alone. Four states—New York, Massachusetts, Illinois,

and Pennsylvania—accounted for half the Y women workers.
Nearly a third of these women were college graduates. Most had
been teachers or office workers, but there were also social workers,
librarians, dietitians, and public health professionals.

Neil M. Heyman, in his book *Daily Life During World War I*,
writes that

> The role of canteen hostesses brought only a small departure from
> a woman's role at home in peacetime. America's YMCA hostesses
> were intended to maintain a soldier's tie with life across the Atlan-
> tic. These women were expected to provide a comfortable resting
> place for soldiers, to give them refreshments and a friendly female
> partner with whom to talk. Implicitly they were to keep soldiers
> away from sordid sexual encounters with French women and the
> accompanying threat of venereal disease. Their own social lives and
> free time were closely supervised and almost all found themselves
> under the hierarchy of male officials.

By fall 1917, it had become accepted that the women in France
were the envoys of the American home front, representatives of
all the women left behind.

In an article in *Ladies Home Journal*, in September 1918, Evan-
geline Booth wrote,

> These women.... are the 'little mothers of the battlefields' whom you
> read about as cooking, mending, singing, praying.... serving hot
> coffee to sentinels in the dead of night and doing what you mothers
> of fighters would do for your boys if YOU were over there.

Work in the canteens could be stressful and tiring. The women
had long hours, from early morning until late in the evening. As

busy as they were, they were urged by their superiors to socialize as much as possible with the men who visited their canteens. This often meant that after a long day's work they were asked to attend dances and were expected to dance with as many men as possible.

Some of the women referred to the "dancing problem," with one reporting that for each dance she was expected to dance with three to seven men.

(Nowhere in any of her correspondence with family members does Elisabeth mention dancing at the canteen.)

Whatever they did, the canteen women were expected to be on their best behavior while offering the troops just the right amount of service, socialization, humor, high spirit, and flirtation.

Their rewards for their efforts?

Many could see themselves as close and important partners with America's fighting men and through that partnership they could believe that they were contributing in the best way they could to an Allied victory in France.

The satisfaction they gained from serving thousands of men on leave from the front lines contributed to their sense of being needed and wanted. The expressions of appreciation from individual soldiers, in letters and in person, were gratefully accepted and motivated the women to continue their work.

Many, including Elisabeth, gained personal pleasure in planning and executing large parties, teas, and receptions at the canteens for "our boys."

It was said later that many of the Y women were disappointed with their service because they believed they had been recruited not for what they could actually do to help in the war effort in France but simply as women—to entertain troops, to keep them away from French women, and to do the domestic sorts of jobs that men in charge thought they were suited for.

Could Elisabeth have harbored such disappointment? Perhaps, but her letters home do not reflect that. She wrote of hard work and long hours but nearly all her messages were positive in tone and seemed to indicate her satisfaction, even enthusiasm, for her assignments.

CHAPTER 16

ELISABETH SERVES IN FRANCE/1917-1919

Elisabeth was forty-nine years old in the spring of 1917. Nowhere in her letters or papers is there any indication that she ever was attracted to a man. But she was drawn to Mercer Johnston. Was it his commitment and devotion to the spread of the Social Gospel? Did his patriotism ignite her spirit and lead her to follow his example? Was she at a time in her life when she needed to go in a different direction and find new challenges and excitement? Or was she, perhaps for the first time in her life, attracted to someone of the opposite gender, someone whom she wanted to follow wherever he might lead her?

Readers can decide for themselves as the story of Elisabeth and Mercer unfolds.

One thing seems certain. She was looking for a way out of her busy life in Baltimore, a life filled to overflowing with commitments to social engagements as well as to Baltimore City's poor and needy. She was looking for a respite, for something new.

Elisabeth's official letter of appointment to the National Surgical Dressings Committee of America was brief and to the point, signed on June 23, 1917, from Mary Hatch Willard, who founded the organization that, in cooperation with the Red Cross, was charged with making bandages for allied troops in France.

> We take pleasure in stating that you have been selected by the National Surgical Dressings Committee of America as a volunteer to go to Paris to take charge of the workroom in our Ouvroir there. As the need for volunteers is most urgent, we trust that you will accept the appointment and will arrange to leave for Paris at the earliest possible date.

In July 1917, Elisabeth traveled to New York City with Mercer Johnston and his wife, Katherine, prior to embarking for France.

Before Elisabeth left Baltimore, the editors of the *Baltimore News* and *Baltimore American* newspapers engaged her to write occasional articles for their papers from France describing her life and adventures there.

These accounts, as well as the numerous letters she wrote to her sister Alice, and to her Aunt Louisa, provide a fascinating chronicle of Elisabeth's service overseas.

On August 21, aboard the *Espagne*, a former Transatlantic French Line cruise ship, now a troopship, headed for Bordeaux: "So far I have seen no U-Boats.... I grant you it is a queer feeling to go to bed at night not knowing when we will be called."

While aboard, Elisabeth wrote an update to the *Baltimore News*, which was published on September 13, 1917.

Trying to convey the mood of those aboard the ship, Elisabeth cited the World War I poet Alan Seeger and his poem, "I Have a Rendezvous With Death." She wrote:

> Some of us at least must in France have a 'rendezvous with death' and it gives a different tone to this voyage than that we have previously

experienced, however often we may have crossed. We do not dwell on the difficulties, but on the opportunities that lie before us.

Elisabeth and the Johnstons had been in France less than a month when Mercer Johnston was discharged from the Ambulance Service. The U.S. Army had taken over the organization and he was above the Army's age limit.

Johnston joined the YMCA as a "secretary," as they were called. The secretaries were assigned to various sites where they could provide canteen services to the troops, either in the city canteens or on the front lines.

Elisabeth wrote that Johnston had received "his marching orders and "will have charge of one of the YMCA outposts in the U.S. Army. It is a man's job [underlined] and it will be both hard and worthwhile. We had hoped all three together, but it did not materialize."

Elisabeth and Katherine moved several times after arriving in France, finally settling in Paris at the Hotel Balzac, 14 rue Balzac, on October 1, "one of the many little French hotels on the Elyses, on the south side near the Etoile with a private bath."

It was not long before Elisabeth began to see, firsthand, the battle scars of the young men who, almost daily, returned by train from fighting at the front for rest and recreation in Paris.

She told Alice about a "réforme," the name given to wounded French soldiers who had recovered from their wounds. Katherine had befriended the wife of a young man who had lost a leg in the Battle of the Marne.

He has learned the trade of shoemaker but it is awfully hard to go about on a peg. We have decided to give him an artificial leg. It costs 600 Francs, which at the present exchange rate is about $10.50. It seems as practical a way as any to see a man on his feet and we are going to let any of our friends help for it isn't one but others in the hospital.

I would rather have any Xmas present take this form. I think the people at home would feel the 'tug' of such a man as this, who doesn't complain, does not pose as a hero, does not ask, but has won a medal—I believe the Croix de Guerre—for saving an officer's life. Pass the word if you have a chance.

Elisabeth spent most of her day wrapping bundles of bandages and she grew restless.

Writing to Alice on October 9:

Mr. Johnston has been only away for a week [with the YMCA] but next week he goes off much farther and nearer the front and may not get leave for three months, which will be hard.

I shall miss him very much, too, for a man's point of view is so delightful.

She said she had learned how to "break the monotony of work and have some quite pleasant people in the wrapping room of which I am now in charge. Life is normal and I only wish I were rendering more service but I hope it will come later."

On October 15, the *Baltimore News* published an account in which Elisabeth seemed determined to give the paper's readers a clear understanding of the important roles women were filling in France.

On all hands we admire the poise and self-control of the women, whether they be those who have met sorrow upon sorrow, by losing their dear ones, or those whom the economic strain has forced into strange and unaccustomed surroundings, or those who are working in hospitals or workrooms for the wounded or in the canteens where at any hour of the day or night, the wounded soldiers are given a hot meal on their arrival at the (rail) station.

There is no pose of the heroic about it, no praise given or expected, but day by day, week by week, year by year, the work has been done and done well.

Later in October, Elisabeth reported to Alice that she had received "a most interesting job offer." She had been invited to work in one of the YMCA canteens in Paris, which were available to servicemen who had been granted temporary leave from the battlefield.

Effective November 1, she would be working in a Y Canteen at the Hotel Pavillon, 30 rue de l'Echiquier. At any one time some 300 to 400 soldiers, sailors, and marines would be in residence. She described her role as "hostess, provider of general information and shopkeeper."

"My work grows daily in interest and I hope...to have such a good corps of women workers that things will blossom under my eyes," she wrote.

Besides working at the Pavilion's newsstand counter "selling tobacco, chocolates and stamps and having little friendly chats with our boys," Elisabeth was also in charge of social events.

Our first tea last Sunday, 4-6, was a howling success. Friends rallied to me and enjoyed it as much as the boys, and we fed about 150 with tea and chocolate cake. We had saved sugar all the previous week. The days are not really long enough for all the opportunities to help our boys. The boys are most appreciative, most of the time, and say very nice things.

Around this time, Elisabeth expanded on her experiences in an account to the Baltimore newspapers.

I would like to take this opportunity of saying what a fine type of men come to us here…We chat with them over the newsstand when they are begging for more cigarettes, or asking whether the latest number of the *Saturday Evening Post* has come over, or delighting in chocolates, which we try to find for them in any quarter of Paris…

Most of the men appreciate the home-like atmosphere of this hotel where there are American women who take friendly interest in them even to sewing on their buttons or telephoning for them in French or guiding them on sight-seeing trips.

In a November 21 letter to Alice, she wrote: "I believe I will be here for the winter at least and am very happy in the work. It takes a bit of ingenuity and tact and energy that I can command—plus devotion to the highest ideals."

She took a soldier shopping. When someone asked him who she was, he answered, "She is everyone's Patron Saint." She said she was not "telling this in a bragging spirit, but you can see how happy I am to be of service to our boys."

During the Christmas season, 1917, Elisabeth told Baltimore readers how she and her "boys" spent Christmas at the Hotel Pavilion.

We may be 4,000 miles away from home in a city near the war zone, and where the chief celebration is New Year's Day, but we have had our own festivities in the good old Baltimore way, and that is, giving everyone from the 'States' just as happy a day as possible.

She described a Christmas Eve party with carols "which never meant more to me as when sung by the well-modulated voices of five hundred soldiers far away from home and about to fight for a righteous peace."

> At the end of the evening the tree was lighted and each man was given a warm sock [containing] the other sock, mandarin nuts, chocolate bonbons, a box of Pall Mall cigarettes, a cigarette holder, and a Christmas card peeping out of the top.
>
> The party broke up but do not let me forget to say that many nice American girls came down to help the older women entertain the men.

She wrote that soldiers had pooled their funds to provide gifts to 100 orphaned French children who had been invited to the hotel to receive gifts and entertainment.

"This gathering made a link in the chain that binds us closer to our friends and allies here in Paris." After the children left an American jazz band "from the Casino arrived to give us the most stirring ragtime music possible."

And that was followed by the presentation of "the marvelous LIBERTY CAKE."

> It weighed 300 pounds, was four feet in diameter, made by the chef at the Waldorf Astoria, re-frosted here in Paris with a Christmas inscription surrounded by red, white and blue flowers and by bags of red, white and blue candy and crowned by a bronze Statue of Liberty made by Gorham & Company. This was the greatest thing of the day.

Writing to Alice, she elaborated: "I was selected to cut the famous Liberty Cake of which you have doubtless read. The boys cheered me as I cut the cake."

The New Year: 1918

Almost from the beginning of her service in Paris, Elisabeth had told Alice of her concern about Katherine Johnston's health. "The work may be tiring her too much" became a familiar phrase in her letters.

Was she trying to assure Alice, who often had expressed concern about Elisabeth's health, that she was in very good health, despite all the work she was doing? Or did Elisabeth see herself as stronger, physically and mentally, than Katherine and perhaps was pleased with herself in that regard?

On February 10, Elisabeth wrote to Alice that despite her grinding schedule, "I have gained almost nine pounds since December. Mrs. J seems better too. Tho' now that Mr. J. has gone to the front it is anxious work. He is very lean and eager to render this particular sort of work for the cause."

Late in February, Katherine left the Surgical Dressings service and joined Elisabeth in her YMCA work, "so we are going to move to a hotel in the neighborhood" of the Pavillon. Instead, the Pavillon manager, Ray Newton, provided accommodations for them at the hotel.

Elisabeth's March 7 letter was interrupted by an air raid "alerte." She found some candles "so we were able to keep the Canteen open till the usual hour, for a few men came despite the excitement and it seemed to me it was steadying to have things go normally."

"One bomb went off nearby comparatively, as perhaps you can make out if you have a map of Paris," she wrote, adding that it would be "indiscreet" to say exactly where it hit, because military censors might not let the letter go through. "At all events, we were not frightened."

In a later letter (March 21), she described a bombing raid:

The sight of the explosion last Friday was wonderfully dreadful but very beautiful—the great pillars of fire and glow, small explosions continuously, the area covered with exploded granules—people quite composed.

On April 14, she wrote about the war:

The anxiety of the great battle is very oppressive for more than any personal danger...from long range Berthas. Till you are here you don't realize how awful the struggle is.

(The German army had launched a spring offensive in late March and moved rapidly, hoping to achieve many victories before a large number of U.S. forces could flood the battlefield. But the Germans were hampered by slow supply lines and the late arrival of reinforcements. Although hard fought battles were still to come, the war was beginning to turn in favor of the Allied Forces.)
April 15:

The big gun woke me up early this a.m. much to my disgust and, as I could not get back to sleep, I am devoting time to correspondence.

I have a good many letters to the boys and to their families at home. I didn't know that I am obliged to do this, but it seems friendly and helpful.

(The "big gun" might have been the so-called Paris Gun, the largest artillery gun of World War I. It went into service in March 1918, and was able to lob its shells into Paris from a distance of 75 miles. Accuracy was poor but the Germans hoped to inflict psychological damage among Parisians.)
"Mr. Johnston's unit has been bombed and I think he is in a good deal of danger, tho' not on the battle front..."

From time to time, Elisabeth told Alice about her circumstances in Paris, which might be construed as dangerous, but Elisabeth seemed to shrug them off.

Elisabeth wrote:

The sounds of war, the Berthas [another large cannon], do not trouble me personally. I have decided to go quietly with my work, and not let my sleep be interfered with more than possible, and so go to bed, instead of to the clear [shelter] when there is a raid, for I consider that lack of sleep is far more to be dreaded than a possible bomb, and our rooms are not high up.

A Summer Respite

Some of the significant battles of the war were taking place during mid-summer of 1918—Second Battle of the Somme, Chateau-Thierry, Soissons.

Yet, in the midst of this, Elisabeth and the Johnstons were granted "permissions" for a three-week vacation.

Writing from Chamonix in the French Alps on July 9, Elisabeth said to Alice, "Now you will have a real letter." It is the longest letter among all those she wrote from France.

"At last we are realizing the rest and delight of a holiday together, Mr. and Mrs. Johnston and I."

One wonders if the Johnstons might have enjoyed some time away, alone. But there are suggestions in later letters that Elisabeth may have been financing the trip. For example: "I wanted to give my friends the nicest sort of time."

She wrote that she was glad they "were not at Aix and to be away from the soldiers for a time. ... Here it seems hard to realize the War. Mt. Blanc is stupendous, dominating everything."

On July 4, Elisabeth and the Johnston's visited Lafayette's grave in Picpus Cemetery, Paris, "where I had never been, for we wanted to have the entire historic setting before us at this time."

She continued:

Mr. Johnston sees it all—historically and spiritually in a very inspiring way—the revelation of America to the cause of Liberty, and the influence of France on our country in this development. I wish you could hear him on this and I would greatly like to see him write it as an essay for the *Atlantic*, but I fear he is physically too tired from the strain of the past year to make him want to do it.

Almost two weeks later, in a letter begun on July 19 and finished on the 22nd, Elisabeth described Mercer Johnston's attempt to climb the highest mountain in the Alps, the 15,780 foot Mt. Blanc:

The hotel guests were immensely interested two days ago when Mr. Johnston made the ascent of Mt. Blanc and almost all day there were relays at the telescope watching for him at different points. The snow was deep on the mountain and the wind stiff and made going far more difficult than usual.

And, she said,

He suffered from the absolute exhaustion which comes from the rarity of the air.

He got within two meters of the summit but had to turn back. It was a tremendous disappointment and the guides wanted to pull him up by ropes but he thought that was too much for them, so he gave up. He had no bad effects and enjoyed tennis yesterday, but I don't think it has left him being keen for other expeditions...

Back at the Pavillon Hotel

By late summer, back to work again at the Hotel Pavillon canteen, Elisabeth had become recognized by her superiors as someone they could depend on to do good work, largely on her own, without their close direction.

In a letter to Alice on August 30, she reported that what had started out to be an ordinary day, "expecting the daily round of duties" turned out to be quite different "when I suddenly was called up from Headquarters of the YMCA to know if I would help organize a new leave area."

> It has been a hurry up call from the Army, and we get there at 6 a.m. Sunday and 200 soldiers are due that day. I am to organize the women's work of the canteen, excursions & entertainments.
>
> Mrs. Theo. Roosevelt, Jr., who organized Aix, will be down the middle of next week and the chairman of the Soldiers' Leave Department of the YMCA. It will be an interesting piece of work, and it is only under agreement that I return here [to the Pavilion] at the end of three weeks that I consented to take it.

On September 18, after being summoned back to Paris for another assignment, she wrote to Alice to explain this latest development. Her new assignment, a temporary one, was "to organize the women's work at the Palace de Glace behind the Grand Palais on the Champs Elysees." It had been a skating center.

> It is a rather drab building but the former rink will be a good auditorium and is planned to have some show going on in it from 2 to 10:30 p.m. The women's work will be to run the refreshment counter.

Elisabeth was not shy about letting her superiors know where she stood regarding her various assignments. In this case: "I only promised to get it on its feet and I stipulated that my strength be saved by sufficient use of automobiles.

> They are really awfully nice to me up at Headquarters and I generally get what I ask for.... Of course we are all overjoyed at the splendid work our boys have done at the Front and I find the French people almost pathetically grateful... I am only sorry that these bits of organization keep me from seeing personally as many boys as I would like.

On November 1, Elisabeth noted it was All Saints Day. She was writing from the Pavilion.

> I am back at my old post at the Pavilion, the Palais de Glace being fairly well launched... It was a very interesting piece of work but I still had the responsibility of the Pavilion and hardly any time to attend it. Besides, the personal work among the boys was almost nil, so I was not altogether sorry to wind it up yesterday at the end of the month and at the end of my year of service with the Y.

In less than two weeks the Great War would end.

> The war is of course drawing to a close .... but dear old sister, don't expect me home when peace is declared, for it will be my duty, I think, to stay over for some time longer.

Perhaps, like the soldiers she was serving, Elisabeth had questions about what direction her life would take after the war. "I can't say what I want to do, but for once in my life it looks as if I would obey the call of the daughter to a sense of duty."

She abruptly changed the subject with this bad news:

We heard tonight that Mr. Johnston has been gassed, but he wrote the telegram himself so it is not alarming, though very bad. Mrs. Johnston is plucky and anxious to get leave to visit him at Limoges.

(Base Hospital 28 was at Limoges and was staffed by physicians, nurses, and other health care workers largely from the University of Kansas School of Medicine. It opened on July 21, 1918. Its facilities included a building formerly occupied by a girls' school, Bellaire Seminary, prefabricated buildings, and tents. The hospital would eventually accommodate 2,900 wounded soldiers.)

The War's End

Elisabeth did not write to Alice on November 11, 1918, the day the Armistice was declared, but she picked up her pen the next day, on the 12th, to give Alice some of the flavor of that exciting, historic day to which she was a witness.

She described "the great and almost mad joy of the Armistice."

I had the car yesterday for business & extended the drive to the Place de la Concorde, so that I might see 'Strassbourg' with her crown of gold." [The statue had been covered with black crepe throughout the war.]

The crowds were enormous & on returning it took about 30 minutes to go two squares…and that night when an opera singer sang the Marseillaise from a balcony of the 'Matin' [newspaper office building] it was hardly safe to be afoot for people were so crushed by the crowd, but I heard it and got home safe.

Reporting to Alice on Mercer's condition following his encounter with a German gas attack, she wrote that "he is making gradual improvement" and he hopes to do Canteen work in the town where he is in the Hospital [Limoges], but he is able to be with her [Mrs. Johnston] a good part of the time and the Doctor promises complete recovery."

Although she was not aware of what the Johnstons' plans would be after he left the hospital, she has her own plans:

> I suppose I shall stay on in Paris for the winter, for more and more boys will be allowed to come here.
>
> We are so crowded now, for the accommodation of the Pavillon is altogether inadequate.

Indeed, just a week after the Armistice was declared, Elisabeth's canteen work may have been busier than it ever was during the war as hundreds of soldiers were given leave to go to Paris. November 18:

> Life is so very strenuous in these days that I hardly know which way to turn. The boys are flocking to Paris…and this hotel is a commissary. It is almost impossible to keep up but we do the best we can.
>
> Added to all else there has been a strike in our 'French help,' and we are on thin ice about our dining room force and many of the kitchen brigade have already gone. I don't worry but it is a bit exciting.
>
> Paris, as I wrote you, went wild with joy and has not yet quite recovered. I am too anxious for the future, with the Kaiser at large now and unstable government in Berlin, to be too exuberant, but I am thankful not to have any more men killed.
>
> There is a restless spirit in the air, but things will go alright, I imagine.

Elisabeth had sought Alice's approval in 1917 for her to go over-
seas to support the war effort and once again she had sought her
approval to remain in France for a while after the war ended.

The day after Christmas (and her 51st birthday), Elisabeth wrote
to Alice:

> I am glad you are satisfied to have me stay over some months more,
> for it seems to me a commonsense thing for those of us who know
> the ropes to keep at it a bit longer.

Wrapping Up in France: January – June 2019

In January 1919, Elisabeth was given a series of assignments outside Paris, at battlefield sites known to most Americans back home:
places like Chateau Thierry, Verdun, and Conflans.

In mid-March, she wrote from Verdun, the site of one of the
longest single battles of the war. It began the third week of February 1916, and was declared ended in the middle of December
that year. There are differing estimates of the loss of life at Verdun.
Some have said that the French lost more than 360,000 soldiers,
the Germans nearly 340,000.

Describing Verdun:

> One feels as if one were living among the ruins of Pompeii, but we
> are living in an old college close to the Cathedral, which fortunately
> has a roof. There are five of us women who are quartered in a long
> dormitory, with plenty of blankets.
>
> I answer questions, give out stationery, register books and make
> myself agreeable in any way …There is little worry over here, no
> funds to raise, few engagements to keep and, best of all, no meet-
> ings to attend.

Her schedule had been reduced to about two or three days a week, "most busy when the troop trains arrive, for example, serving 450 men in about 35 to 40 minutes."

Toward the end of March 1919, Elisabeth began to show signs of restlessness, fatigue, and irritability. Noting, in a letter to Alice on March 19, that she had been in France for 19 months, she said that her work was "much easier than it has been, yet I feel it much more—not an actual fatigue but in a general feeling of stupidity."

Later in the month, she suggested, for the first time, a possible departure date. "I suppose it will be August."

"You see I am already beginning to look homeward ... I don't want to go back to the same old rut however good the rut was."

Over the next weeks and months, she worked at a Canteen in Romagne, then came back to Verdun, and then to Conflans in late April, where she worked harder than ever.

Although it is not clear exactly when Elisabeth received her orders to leave Conflans for Paris, it seems to have been toward the end of May 1919.

In late May, shortly before she left France, Elisabeth received a YMCA memorandum praising her service in the Verdun region. The Y Secretary for Verdun, A.N. Gay, wrote to Ella Sachs at the Women's Bureau, YMCA, in Paris to tell her of the esteem in which he held Elisabeth.

He said she had arrived with recommendations that had spoken of her "in glowing terms" but he had wondered if "all the good things.... could possibly be true." But, "as time went on," he said, they were. He concluded the correspondence with this: "We are mighty glad to have had Miss Gilman with us and assure you that her influence has been felt and that her share of credit for the success of our organization was no small one."

In early June 1919, Elisabeth received a one-page, military-like discharge from the Personnel Department of the Women's Bureau of the Y.

Dated June 2, it stated that "Miss Elisabeth Gilman has been given an honorable discharge" for service begun November 1, 1917, and that she would be leaving Paris on June 6 "for Boulogne to go to England and thence to the USA."

CHAPTER 17

BUILDING STEAM WITH PROGRESSIVE CAUSES

I f newspaper articles from Fall 1919 are to be relied upon, Elisabeth seems to have taken about two months to resettle at home on Park Avenue, see her old friends, and then move swiftly into a social and political whirlwind that would define her life for the next 30 years.

A letter to the Johnstons on September 22: "My first night at home. Here I am, with my two boys, Page and Woolsey [students], with Stewart [servant] in attendance and Charlotte [servant] in prospect and mighty nice it is..."

Elisabeth joined the Baltimore Committee of The Women's Trade Union League of America. One November evening the Committee held a public meeting before a packed audience at Ford's Opera House on West Fayette Street. Its special guests were Margaret Bondfield, a British trade unionist and member of Parliament who later would become the first woman cabinet member as Minister of Labour; and Tom Shaw, also a labor member of the British Parliament and secretary of the International Textile Workers Union.

Civic leaders asked her to help the Baltimore Alliance, a social service organization. She met with them on January 20, 1920, at a luncheon at The Southern Hotel to launch a campaign for $500,000 to help underwrite the work of the Alliance.

Elisabeth was among friends. Reporting on the accomplishments of the Alliance, so far, and soliciting for more funds was B. Howell Griswold, Jr., a Johns Hopkins alumnus (1894) and a trustee of the University. Another member was her old friend Joseph S. Ames, the Hopkins physics professor.

In 1919, a group of progressives met in New York to create an organization that might lead to the birth of a third political party in the United States, a party whose platform would counteract the increasing conservatism of both the Democrat and Republican parties but also would eschew the growing pro-communist movements in the country.

It was called the Committee of Forty-Eight. Its first published statement said, in part:

> It is the purpose of the Committee of Forty-Eight to summon from all parts of the country the leaders of its liberal thought and its forward-looking citizens, to meet in conference. We hope that out of this assemblage of the scattered forces of Americanism will come a flexible statement of principles and methods that will permit effective cooperation with organized Labor and Agricultural workers in the tasks of social reconstruction.

Some 500 people attended the organizing conference in St. Louis on December 9-12, 1919. The adopted platform, among other things, called for public ownership of transportation, stockyards, grain elevators, public utilities and coal, oil, natural gas and mineral deposits, and timber and water works.

Elisabeth, together with her friends Mercer Johnston, Richard Hogue, William Cochran, and others met as an executive committee to establish the Maryland chapter of the Committee of Forty-Eight on March 3, 1920. Johnston was the chairman, Cochran the treasurer, and Elisabeth the secretary. Headquarters for the committee were at 513 Park Avenue.

The *Sun*, in its March 4 edition, said the group had set itself a task of "welding the liberal forces of the country into a complete body and possibly into a political body."

Strong efforts were made between 1920 and 1922 to unify the various liberal factions, to knit them into a single, powerful political movement, but within a relatively short time critical differences arose among the "Forty-Eighters," the Labor Party, and other Progressives.

The committee did, however, play an important role in enabling Robert M. LaFollette, Sr., a United States Senator from Wisconsin, to become the Progressive Party's presidential candidate in 1924.

Elisabeth was a strong supporter of the Progressive Party that year and in her informal memoir, she wrote: "In 1923 I became head of the Women's Division of the LaFollette-Wheeler Presidential campaign and was an elector on that ticket." (Wheeler was Montana's U.S. Senator, Burton K. Wheeler.)

Throughout the 1920s, Elisabeth was a prominent spokesperson for progressive causes. She and her colleagues received significant media coverage for their activities.

During that time she helped to establish the Maryland Chapter of the American Civil Liberties Union. In 1921, she held a meeting at her home, to create the Maryland Civil Liberties Committee. Ten years later, in 1931, the Maryland Chapter of the American Civil Liberties Union was launched at 513 Park Avenue.

The West Virginia Miners Strike
During the spring of 1922, Elisabeth focused nearly every waking

moment of her life on assisting destitute miners and their families in West Virginia. The men had been unable to work because of an extended strike.

In her memoir, Elisabeth reported that she issued a mass appeal for funds to assist those on strike. That appeal was issued April 15, 1922, and it captured the essence of her efforts.

It was written on 513 Park Avenue letterhead. She is listed as "Secretary Treasurer of the West Virginia Miners Relief Association." Excerpts:

We are at a crucial moment in our country's history, for the Union Miners face disorganization unless they win the strike.

They stand for a minimum week of 30 hours, so that their wage may be stabilized on a yearly basis. They MUST win, and to do this they must live as individuals, and for this, food in large quantities is absolutely necessary. You believe this, don't you?

Our believing friends gave us last week five carloads of food, 265,000 pounds of flour, meat, beans etc. on condition that we pay the freight to the New River field. We are the only committee sending food there, and we could not tell the 40,000 men, women and children dependent on us to starve.

Elisabeth was seeking about $3,400 in this appeal—$1,400 for freight charges "and $2,000 for FOOD for our next shipment."

She wrote in her memoir that she also sought funds, nationally, by taking out a large advertisement in *The New York Times*.

Throughout May, Elisabeth received letters and telegrams about the needs of the miners. She was raising money, dispensing money, and keeping meticulous account of each penny received and dispensed.

She asked Mercer Johnston to help with her efforts. Letters

between them were brief, staccato-like, overflowing with commitment to the cause.

That summer she continued her efforts to aid the strikers from the family home in Norwich, while Mercer and Katherine Johnston, at her invitation, moved in to her home at 513 Park Avenue.

"I hope that you like the big house for your summer abiding place and that you are both feeling well."

(Part of Elisabeth's reason for going to Norwich was to be with Aunty Lou, who was in failing health. Louisa died in early August. Responding to the Johnstons' messages of sympathy, Elisabeth said she was happy to have been at her side when she died. "To go so far down in the Valley of the Shadow," she wrote, "is one of the ways our Lord teaches us the path, don't you think?")

The West Virginia coal strike was settled that summer. Elisabeth called it a "comparatively just settlement that [John L.] Lewis has made. It will be interesting to see if the New River Coal Company conforms & if so when."

On November 1, Elisabeth published a formal "Report of West Virginia Miners Relief Committee." The report showed cash receipts of $21,781, plus in-kind gifts of food, clothing, and costs of freight. Expenditures were the same, making a break-even operation.

However, the document said that the strike had continued because the coal company refused to sign the agreement, which resulted in putting the mines back into operation but leaving some 600 miners and their families "blacklisted" and out of work "because they were the ones who stood out most valiantly for the end. They and their families are stranded in an unfriendly county, living in tents and tar-paper shacks without the possibility of work or the means to move."

She said, "We are appealing to you once more to tell them you are with them in a way that will count for them and the cause of Organized Labor." Recipients were asked to send their donations to Elisabeth at 513 Park Avenue.

Advocating for Immigrants, the Old, and the Young

The Washington Bureau of the *Baltimore Sun* reported on March 25, 1926, that Elisabeth appeared before the House Immigration Committee to criticize Congressional plans to register aliens and to extend provisions of the existing deportation law. A University of Chicago professor and a former federal prosecutor from Philadelphia, representing the ACLU, joined her.

Mercer Johnston accompanied her to Washington. Although he did not testify, as she did, he left a statement with the committee opposing their proposed actions.

In early February 1927, Elisabeth and the most socially active, reform-minded faculty member at Johns Hopkins, Dr. Broadus Mitchell, were invited to represent Maryland at a New York conference to discuss forming a permanent organization to work for old-age pensions.

They were among a group of 100 individuals from throughout the country who, according to the *Sun*, "included members of Congress and others of widely divergent political views." They had been invited by Dr. Abraham Epstein, an economist who is remembered today as the person who introduced the phrase "Social Security."

In the mid-1920s, Elisabeth was secretary of an organization that the *Sun* described as "the Pioneer Youth" movement. Most likely it was a group that organized in several states and was known as The Young Pioneers of America (YPA).

The YPA was a children's organization affiliated with the Communist Party of the United States. It recruited children from eight or ten years old to about sixteen and it was generally associated with a school or a particular neighborhood. Meetings were held in labor halls or local workers' centers owned by Communist affiliated groups. Its purpose was to introduce children to the precepts of communism.

Among the YPA's most successful programs were its summer camps, of which about twenty existed around the country between 1925 and 1930. On June 2, 1927, the *Sun* reported that Elisabeth had announced the opening of a "Pioneer Youth" camp at Fort Smallwood in Anne Arundel County, just south of Baltimore. The camp, to accommodate twenty-five boys and girls, would open July 1 and run for two months. It would be called the Henry F. Broening Camp. (Broening was the president of the Baltimore Federation of Labor.)

There is no record that the camp continued after 1927, and the national YPA movement disbanded in 1934.

Toward the end of November 1928, Elisabeth was serving on yet another committee, with leaders including Mercer Johnston. This time it was a group known as the Save Our Schools (SOS) Committee, a national body of distinguished citizens who had come together to fight what they believed to be undue influence in schools and colleges by privately held utility companies that feared government ownership of their businesses.

The *Baltimore Sun* reported on November 19 that the committee was headed by Methodist Bishop Francis J. McConnell, a former president of DePauw University and a social reformer with special interests in industrial democracy, social security, and civil rights.

The vice chairman was John Dewey of Columbia University, well known then, and today, for his promotion of progressive education and its significance in a democratic society.

Johnston was secretary of the SOS and a spokesman.

Elisabeth was among 70 members of the committee. Some

others were Jane Addams, one of the period's leading advocates for
social reform and founder of the settlement house, Hull House, in
Chicago; William Allen White, the Pulitzer Prize-winning editor
of the *Emporia* (Kansas) *Gazette*; Professor Felix Frankfurter,
then of the Harvard Law School; Mary Woolley, president of Mt.
Holyoke College; and Oswald Villard, editor of *The Nation*.

Elisabeth's listing among committee members identified her
as a resident of Baltimore and, yet once again, the daughter of
Daniel C. Gilman, former president of Johns Hopkins University.

CHAPTER 18

THE OPEN FORUM IN BALTIMORE

Elisabeth's newspaper accounts of her experiences in France kept her name before the public during the war years. After she returned home to Baltimore in 1919, she became a leader in the city's popular Open Forum, a weekly series of Sunday afternoon lectures held between November and April. They attracted large, mostly liberal-leaning, audiences.

From the beginning Elisabeth played a major role in the Forums, initially as the organization's first treasurer, later its secretary and, after two of the directors left Baltimore, as she put it in her memoir, "it fell to my lot to be the Director."

The Baltimore *Sun*, on March 30, 1915, in the first announcement of the intent to create the Forum, reported that it would provide a venue "where all questions relating to human welfare can be freely discussed and where prominent speakers from all over the country can appear to speak on these subjects."

The rector of Baltimore's Episcopal Church of the Ascension, the Rev. Dr. R. W. Hogue, was the moving force in creating the Open Forum. He already had experience in running a similar speakers' series at his church at Lafayette and Arlington Avenues. The *Sun* described Hogue's program as a "live force" at the church and speculated that with his leadership the city "might soon be able to boast a large downtown forum."

But those programs got Hogue into trouble with his Vestry, the governing body of an Episcopal Church. The Forum's speakers and their messages were much too liberal, too progressive, for the church leaders. The Vestry forced him to resign.

Rev. Hogue had a model, in Boston, for the kind of series he hoped to begin in Baltimore.

In February 1908, a Boston businessman and leader of that city's Baptist Social Union, George W. Coleman, had established a "free speech organization" known as the Ford Hall Forum, with public lectures held in the Social Union's meeting hall on Beacon Hill. Its purpose was to enable local citizens to hear from civic, religious, educational, and cultural leaders of the day and "to enable the full, free, open discussion of all vital questions affecting human welfare."

It was exactly what Dr. Hogue hoped to establish in Baltimore.

(The Ford Hall Forum continues to operate in Boston as a community service of Suffolk University. The Baptist Social Union also is active in the Boston area, operating as "a Christian fellowship of men promoting love among all people." Its mission is to provide financial support to "worthy ministries in the Boston area.")

The Baltimore Open Forum was held at various theaters and public meeting halls in the city. Sometimes meetings were moved to a new location because an existing site could no longer accommodate larger audiences. On a few occasions the buildings' owners ejected the Forum because they did not like the rowdiness that occurred when troublemakers infiltrated the audience to protest some speakers' points of view.

Some of the buildings where Open Forum was held are still

standing, although not all are used for the same purpose as they were at the time.

They include: Royal Arcanum Hall, 18 W. Saratoga St.; Auditorium Theater, Howard and Preston Streets; Hippodrome Theater, 12 N. Eutaw; Colonial Theater, Washington and Gay Streets; The Academy of Music, 516 N. Howard St.; and Victoria Theater, 415 E. Baltimore St.

The first account of an Open Forum presentation appeared in the *Sun* on November 11, 1916. It announced that Rev. Mercer Green Johnston would speak the following day, a Sunday, at 3 p.m. at the Academy of Music.

Prior to the Open Forum, he told the *Sun*, he would speak on, "Why I became a Socialist." If the audience had come to the Academy of Music on that Sunday afternoon hoping to hear an emotional, fire-and-brimstone address, they were not disappointed. "I am not a mere reformer," Johnston said. "I am a revolutionist." He added, "The social monster of capitalism is alone responsible for the horrors of our social conditions."

> Compromise is useless—dickering is useless. There is only one way to wipe out the abjectness of our social conditions—and that is to take from capitalism the things that capitalism has wrongfully acquired from the people.

Perhaps Elisabeth had Johnston's remarks in mind when she wrote some years later that while she had not declared herself a Socialist prior to World War I, she knew in her heart that she embraced the principles of Socialism.

Liberals, radicals, social reformers, and suffragists quickly followed Johnston to the stage of the Open Forum in late 1916 and early 1917.

On December 9, Scott Nearing, a University of Pennsylvania-trained economist, was the speaker. He had been on the faculty at Penn but before coming to Baltimore he had been dismissed for his public expression of his radical ideas, an action the historian, Stephen J. Whitfield called "the most famous breach of academic freedom of the era."

A week after Nearing's appearance, it was Rose Pastor Stokes, who later would become one of the founders of the Communist Party in the United States. On this trip to the Open Forum she was known as a social activist who, although a Jewish Russian immigrant, had met and married a prominent, wealthy New Yorker and active Episcopalian, James Graham Phelps Stokes. He was a leader in New York's settlement house movement.

In her talk, as reported by the *Sun* on December 19, Pastor Stokes lamented the fact that women were saddled by so many domestic chores that they were not able to participate fully in addressing the social and political issues of the day. The *Sun's* reporter ridiculed her talk with this conclusion to his article:

> We do not know how the suffragist ladies will relish the statement [by Pastor Stokes] that 'the female of the species is 500 years behind the male' [because she is tied down by domestic demands]. We are inclined to think she is quite abreast of him in many respects, and ahead of him in others…and that she will not like the comparison made by her socialistic champion.

Mercer Johnston was back again at the Academy of Music speaking on April 1, 1917. His topic was "Patriotism and Radicalism." He described himself as a pro-war radical. However, his views were not those held by Dr. Hogue or the majority of the audience. The *Sun* described questions to Johnston as "highly accusatory, but the meeting was orderly."

That was not the case later that evening when the former president of Stanford University, David Starr Jordan, a well-known pacifist, was in Baltimore to give an anti-war speech, also at the Academy of Music. Here is how the *Sun* reported the evening event:

> The temper of the town could not brook this [promotion of pacifism] and a small mob of ardent anti-pacifists raided this meeting. The police tried to stop the crowd but some heads were cracked. The meeting was broken up and Dr. Jordan left hurriedly. The owners of the Academy became alarmed and refused to house either the Forum or the Community Service any longer.

When the United States entered World War I in 1917, the Open Forum was temporarily discontinued. Mercer Johnston was the final speaker, in April of that year, the same month in which the country declared war on Germany.

The Open Forum meetings resumed on January 4, 1920. Rev. Hogue returned to his position as director of the Forum.

(Later that year Hogue became executive secretary of the Church League of Industrial Democracy and moved to Philadelphia, the League's headquarters. The League had been founded a year earlier by Vida Dutton Scudder, the Episcopalian and Wellesley professor whose remarks at a church conference in 1916 had introduced Elisabeth to Socialism. Mercer Johnston succeeded Hogue as director of the Open Forum. Elisabeth was Secretary. When Johnston resigned, Elisabeth became director.)

When the Forum resumed on that Sunday afternoon in January at the Colonial Theater, Mercer Johnston was the speaker once again. He picked up where he had left off in the spring of 1917.

He condemned U.S. Attorney General A. Mitchell Palmer for

having arrested, between 1917 and 1919, some 600 persons Palmer identified as anarchists. He had deported 60 of them. In subsequent months, as many as 4,000 were arrested in 33 cities and 500 were deported. Johnston called the actions "shameful and un-American."

He also urged the creation of a Liberal Party to move political forces outside of what he called the "mis-representative" Republican and Democrat parties.

"I am an American, born and bred," he concluded. "Nothing but the Cross is more sacred to me than the Stars and Stripes. And I say that if we Americans do not get together on a simple and definite fighting platform we will be deprived of our rights and cried down by those who are not as American as we are."

Not everyone in Baltimore supported the kind of free speech espoused at the Open Forum presentations.

On January 11, 1920, Hogue and the speaker of the day, Harriett Stanton Blatch, a New York suffrage leader, arrived at the Colonial Theater at Washington and Gay Streets to find that someone opposed to suffrage had made sure the door was locked. When they finally got inside the hall it had no heat. Hogue quickly searched for other venues but, finding none, announced that Mrs. Blatch would speak "here and now, robbing the 'antisuffs' of a good laugh at our expense," according to a *Sun* report.

Blatch was the daughter of the famous American suffragette, Elizabeth Cady Stanton. She was a Socialist candidate for public office in the 1920s, ten years before Elisabeth would represent the Socialist Party on election ballots.

Throughout the 1920s, dozens of speakers, mostly favoring liberal causes, spoke on the widest range of topics. Some examples from the *Sun* headlines, for each of the Open Forum meetings, suggested the speakers' subjects:

"Unrest is Not New; Sees a Real Third Party; Lectures on Child

Welfare; Gives Armenia's Message; France Stung, Disappointed Over Peace Treaty; Scores State Sedition Bill; Advocates Early Marriage; Urges U.S. to Intervene on Ireland's Behalf; Scores Alien Segregation; Liberalism is Growing; Hits Private Profit in Mining of Coal; Arkansas Mob Rule Blamed on Railway; Says World Peace Depends on Labor; Capitalism Passing Declares Speaker (Norman Thomas); Senator (Burton K. Wheeler) Attacks Policy of Government Toward Soviet; Calls Bureaucracy Real Danger to U.S.; Urges West Deal With China Fairly; Calls Democracy's Stock At Low Ebb."

On several occasions Elisabeth's leadership of the Open Forum was praised by speakers and editorial writers.

The Baltimore News, on its editorial page, summed up the 1928-1929 Open Forum season, saying it "was one of the most successful in the Forum's long history. Eighteen meetings were held with an average attendance of more than 900. Accomplished without a financial deficit.

While the Forum committee deserves great credit for making this 'post-graduate' college possible, the dominating figure in Forum affairs has been Miss Elisabeth Gilman, its secretary and for the past season its director.

The editorial went on to endorse a tribute Elisabeth had received from one Charles W. Irvin of New York who said, "The only really fitting tribute that could be paid to her would have to come from all the organizations she has served tirelessly throughout the country in the interests of all humanity."

"Which sentiment," the editorial writer said, "the *News* echoes, in behalf of all its readers."

The Open Forum was attracting larger crowds by the end of the 1920s and early 1930s. It was "the place to go" on Sunday afternoons in Baltimore, especially for people interested in liberal politics.

Because of larger attendance it was moved to the Lyric Theater for its 1932-1933 season. Elisabeth, by then director of the Forum, announced speakers for the coming months. Among them were:

Leaders of the Republican, Democratic and Socialist parties who would be speaking and responding to questions two days before the November 1932 elections; Sherwood Eddy, a religious leader and recent convert to Socialism; Agnes Macphail, the only woman in Canada's Parliament; Fritz Kunz, former head of India's Buddhist College; Fenner Brockway, head of Britain's Independent Labor Party; Margaret Sanger, the birth control advocate; and Edith Wynne Matthison, Shakespearean actress.

Throughout the 1930s, Elisabeth devoted much of her time to fund-raising for the Open Forum. Here is a sample of a solicitation she circulated in October 1938:

> Once again we are writing to urge supporters and well-wishers of Baltimore Open Forum. We need financial support; we need good attendance; we need publicity; so that the prestige and effectiveness of our meetings may grow during this year of turmoil both at home and abroad.
>
> We must more and more do everything possible to maintain our liberties—civil, religious, political—for we find controlled press, controlled speech, rampant all over Europe and also we have many evidences of it in our own country.
>
> We can no longer say that Europe's business is not our business. Sooner or later forces in Europe may make it our business. And when and if that day comes you may look back upon the free days of 1938 and wonder why you didn't do more about it.
>
> Now is the chance to do more about it. Now is the chance to give

the other fellow a chance to say what he thinks so that you yourself may continue to have the right to say what you think!

So in the face of all that is occurring in the world we hope that you will feel that a contribution to the Forum is more than a duty—that it is an obligation you welcome and are glad to fulfill...

By early 1942, there was a consensus among Forum committee members, led by Elisabeth, that the Forum needed to make some changes if it was going to remain vital in the Baltimore community. She invited members to meet at her home on March 24.

Her invitation said the Forum "now in its twenty-second year is faced with a number of important problems in connection with its future operation."

The committee, she said, should consider "having only six speakers in a larger downtown hall and charging 25 cents admission." But, more importantly, she asked that they be prepared to discuss having the Forum presented "as a radio feature, abandoning the public meetings."

The committee voted to pursue the radio route and, on May 11, wrote to "Friends of the Forum."

To keep the Baltimore Open Forum vital in the City's intellectual life, several important changes for the 1942-43 season are under advisement. First, there is a proposal to 'go on the air.' This can be done for three quarters of an hour starting at 3 p.m. on Sundays for approximately $38 over station WITH. The studio will seat 75 comfortably...

The number of programs should be reduced to 6 or 8. The speaker should be garnered in Baltimore or Washington and that something like a Baltimore Discussion Group be broadcast rather than a single speaker.

She said the Forum had only $75 in its bank account and that it would not be receiving the annual donation from the Christian Social Justice Fund.

She asked for "a gift or pledge of $10 now."

The first Open Forum radio presentation was broadcast on Sunday, November 22, 1942, at 8:30 p.m. on WITH, 7 East Lexington Street.

In 1943 the Open Forum was presented on WBAL, Sundays, 5:15 to 5:45 p.m. Each program cost $200 and Elisabeth was soliciting the public for "liberal donations."

It is not clear when the Open Forum faded from the airwaves. It probably became too expensive to maintain. It also is likely that its followers' interests had shifted dramatically from the liberal causes of the 1920s and 1930s to the nation's complete commitment to winning World War II.

CHAPTER 19

PATRON OF MERCER JOHNSTON

Elisabeth's support for Mercer Johnston was anchored in her religious beliefs, in her constant desire to be "practical," and in her emotions.

Mercer was a war hero when he returned to the United States in 1919. He had distinguished himself in combat even though he was a YMCA volunteer.

He was awarded the Distinguished Service Cross for extraordinary assistance he gave to U.S. troops in the middle of a massive bombardment near Verdun in October, 1918. The French Government awarded him the Croix de Guerre.

Despite these courageous achievements, when he came home he was adrift. He had no pulpit from which to broadcast his liberal views, no base from which to advance the Social Gospel. Elisabeth encouraged him to write and speak wherever he could. She was certain that if anyone could awaken the country to the plight of working men and women and their families, he could.

But Mercer and Katherine had a serious problem. They had almost no money. He had borrowed from his father and, in his letters to him, he often apologized that he was unable to pay him back.

On the other hand, Elisabeth was the beneficiary of "family money." As a result, throughout her life she was a generous donor to causes that "addressed the Kingdom of God on Earth," as she often put it.

Mercer and Katherine became one of those "causes."

Correspondence and other materials in the Mercer Green Johnston Papers in the Library of Congress make it abundantly clear that Elisabeth saw herself as patron to the Johnstons, especially Mercer. Her financial support began several years earlier, just a month after she met him.

October 23, 1916: She wrote to tell him she was opening a bank account with a $1,000 deposit. He could use the funds to publish speeches, sermons, or whatever he would like. "I will put in $500...and the other half...later. If anything should happen before I should pay up, there would be a draw on my estate." (For whatever reason, in subsequent years, when pledging money to Mercer, she would remind him that if she should die, her estate would make good on her pledge. Where this deep-seated fear of an early death came from is unclear, but it may have been rooted in her recollection of how close she came to death as a young girl back in New Haven when she was so ill with meningitis.)

Mercer expressed deep gratitude for her gift and she replied to him on October 28, 1916:

It pleases me so much for you to feel so, too, but I do have dollars and cents built into our friendship, so please let us forget who happened to be able to do that part. The brains and the spirit to have a right judgment in its use and scope are a far, far more important part of 'the adventure.'

February 17, 1917: Elisabeth assigned a life insurance policy to the Johnstons. Writing in pencil on a New York Life Insurance Company envelope, which contained the policy she said: "On February 23, 1923, or on my death, this policy is to be handed to Rev. Mercer G. Johnston or his wife, Katherine A. Johnston, as the policy has been assigned to them both as a token of the friendship and of my sympathy with their work in behalf of the Kingdom of Christ. Made February 16, 1917. Elisabeth Gilman."

Letter from Elisabeth to Mercer (both in France) April 17, 1918. "As you know Katherine's signature is also on my letter of credit so she can draw on it...and her expenses over here are a charge on my estate..."

Immediately after Elisabeth returned home in 1919, she began corresponding with Mercer frequently about money matters. September 17, 1919:

> I went to the Safe Deposit yesterday for the first time and mailed (registered) to you two bank books, as you asked, and cut off the four coupons and deposited them at the Colonial Trust. If you are going to keep the bonds as an investment, let me know.

One Big Brotherhood Fund

A major financial development occurred about the same time. Elisabeth and Mercer created what they called "The One Big Brotherhood Fund." She said it was to establish "The Kingdom on Earth of The Just One." Elisabeth would supply the funding for it. In reality the OBB Fund was a device to support Mercer and Katherine so that he could devote himself to speaking and writing, two things Elisabeth constantly urged him to do.

The Elisabeth-Mercer relationship grew more complicated as months passed.

On the one hand they had a close friendship. On the other, they had created a sort of business relationship insofar as the Johnstons' finances were concerned. Into that mix, it does not take much imagination to see how Elisabeth had inserted herself deeply into the fabric of the couple's lives.

Intentionally or not, through frequent suggestions and advice, and through financial support, she seemed to be trying to control the Johnstons.

Take this situation as an example: Mercer considered a job with the Social Democratic League of America in New York. Elisabeth was the Secretary of that organization's "Collegiate Department," whose address was at her home, 513 Park Avenue, Baltimore. When she learned that he was interested in that position, she wrote to him on October 9, 1919. She had checked out the "leadership" of the organization and wondered if they "are fully committed."

Don't promise anything until you have talked with the group. None of them receives a salary. As I see it, if the Fund (our Fund I mean) is to pay your salary it would be best to have it paid to you and not to the League for you [underlined].

She had some more advice for him. Mercer had spoken at various venues around the country. On October 29, 1919, in a "Dear Friends" letter to Mercer and Katherine, she said that she had received postcards from them while they were in Chicago. She also had read an interview he had given in that city. She called it "certainly interesting, but you will not mind if I say that I am afraid a little imp jumped in making you refer to the House of Bishops meeting as 'a distinctly middle class gathering.'

"I am not disputing the fact, but I think a thing like that raises more antagonism than insistence on really vital reforms as we see them, and does not do any good."

Holmes Avenue, a Magazine Venture, and Other Activities

In the 1920s, especially the early years of that decade, Elisabeth and Mercer carried on an extensive correspondence about many matters. She provided funds to help support him and Katherine. She advised him on a magazine venture he was exploring. She had invited Mercer and Katherine to live at her home at 513 Park Avenue, Baltimore. She bought a house on Holmes Avenue in the city where the Johnstons could live.

1920

On May 26, 1920, Elisabeth wrote to her attorney, Herbert H. Brune (Brown, Marshall, Brune & Parker 841-85 Calvert Building, Baltimore). She provided a list of financial obligations "for which I have made myself responsible—all gifts to organizations except one for Mercer Johnston at $1,200 ... I want you to know why I have had the pleasure and privilege of doing the last mentioned during the current year.

> Mr. Johnston has a very rare and individual spiritual gift of leadership and vitalizing religion, and I was in this way enabling him to use these gifts instead of being tied down to less useful lines, as would have been the case had he accepted other positions that were offered to him.
>
> As you know, Mr. and Mrs. Johnston are my very dear friends, to whom I owe a great deal, but this particular arrangement was not primarily for that reason but to free him to work untrammeled for God's Kingdom on Earth.

In August 1920, Elisabeth was in Norwich recovering from a hospital stay for an undisclosed condition.

On August 31, she wrote to Mercer about his interest in

publishing a magazine as a vehicle through which he could express his views and those of other like-minded writers. Elisabeth always had imagined him spreading the Social Gospel through powerful preaching and public speaking. She had not thought he might want to create a magazine. She was cautious.

> Your decision is surely wise to go slowly.... for many reasons. Surely Religion is your major, but whether from the pulpit or from the desk remains to be seen. If, as you suggested, the life of our Lord would appear in our magazine, that in itself would justify the venture.
>
> Of course I realized that you would put your whole self into God's venture and that was why I wanted you to be quite sure that you felt it to be in your best sphere.
>
> The 'voices' calling you may be more distinct before we have a face to face talk and you are willing (if you are then willing!) to tell me more about them.

(She was away and Mercer and Katherine were about to move to 513 Park Avenue.)

> Be sure to use 513 and Stewart (servant) for all they are worth in the moving which at best will be a hard job. I will have the phone connected again and hope you will keep house at least for breakfast and tea.

In the midst of the more serious correspondence was a letter Elisabeth wrote to Mercer on September 9, 1920. It provided some comic relief from the detailed, business-like letters they had been exchanging. It concerned a visit to her sister, Alice, at her home at 153 East 72nd Street in New York City. More importantly it shed light on her relationship with Alice's husband, a wealthy, conservative attorney, Everett P. Wheeler.

Wheeler was a curious mix of a conservative but socially conscious Democrat. He was a highly successful lawyer in New York and one of the founders of the American Bar Association. He also was a founder of New York's Citizens Union, a government watchdog agency, as well as East Side Settlement, an organization that opened its doors in 1891 and continues today to provide social services to some 10,000 New Yorkers annually. In 1894, Wheeler ran for Governor of New York with a party that had left the Democratic Party and was known as the Democratic Reform Party. He received only 27,000 votes.

Much to Elisabeth's chagrin, her brother-in-law was an outspoken advocate for anti-suffragists, a movement Elisabeth railed against until women were allowed to vote. Elisabeth and Everett had had limited correspondence starting in 1916. They were at opposite ends of the political spectrum and neither was shy about expressing strongly held views.

In early 1917, Elisabeth concluded a long letter refuting his conservative stance on current political matters this way: "I do not believe that you and I had better go on discussing this thing (politics) by letter, for it is not very satisfactory, but I will be glad of the opportunity of thinking out some of these problems."

Now, from Alice's home she wrote to Mercer:

I have been here 24 hours, which is one-tenth of my visit, without a collision. I hang out mental red and green danger-beware-lamps and think up subjects on which we may agree, and have offered to cut out his newspaper articles, as he kindly lets me cut out what interests me.

So perhaps you have reformed me—wouldn't my sister be surprised if she knew that—which thought keeps me in a whimsical and therefore amiable temper.

She once again mentioned Mercer's desire to start a magazine. While in New York, she had visited with her former YMCA colleague at the Pavilion in Paris, Ray Newton. "I told him of the possibility of our magazine and if I wanted him to do so he will put me in touch, when I next go through New York, with two or three people who would advise us on the practical side."

On September 20, she wrote Mercer from Norwich to share her thoughts, once again, about the proposed magazine: "I want to be sure, as sure as we humans can reasonably expect to be that it is really the best venture for you to make to God."

It would be a different path than one Elisabeth had envisioned for Mercer but she was willing to move ahead with him even if it did not work out as planned.

> I would not consider that we had failed no matter what the ledger might show. But it is up to us to make it a success as a power. Do you feel within you that we can? I am perfectly willing to sink, if need be, the $5,000, but will that do for a long enough period to carry us through the experimental stage?

She concluded the eight-page letter:

> I can't end this discursive letter without telling you that I will do my best in this fight for God and that I do appreciate very deeply the confidence you have shown in wanting to have me in it. If this is what you consider your best mode of expression, let's do it, if it is in any way possible.

House on Holmes Avenue

While she was thinking about the magazine venture, dealing with her brother-in-law, making sure Mercer and Katherine were comfortable at 513 Park Avenue, and making financial gifts to them, she was working on an arrangement to purchase a house for them.

On September 9, her attorney, Herbert Brune, wrote to her in New Hamburg, where she was visiting with Alice. He reported,

> The securities were sold for you to pay for your purchase of Holmes Avenue…
>
> The Holmes Avenue transaction went through today…I am sending the lease to Mr. Johnston from you, in duplicate, to be passed on by you before sending to him for execution and, if you approve, for your signature on both copies.

She sent the papers to Mercer. "If they are satisfactory to you just keep both copies till I return, after I have signed them. If not, don't sign them and we will readjust to suit you."

By the end of December 1920, the Johnstons had moved from her home at 513 Park Avenue to their new house at 3420 Holmes Avenue. In an undated letter, Elisabeth wrote to thank them for holding "a service" at her home. (Most likely it was a Blessing of the Home service provided for in the liturgy of the Episcopal Church.)

> Sunday night. Dear Friends, It is late but my day would not be complete without telling you how inspiring the service was. I felt it was a dedication of 513 as well as 3420 for they are both 'our homes' ready for our Master's use. Just how and when He will show us His way. I confess to missing you dreadfully but I know it is better thus and it is good to see what a lovely home you have created.

"Any part that I may have in this is the outward token of our friendship which God has surely blessed these past years. Today

is a milestone and I do wonder how He will answer our earnest
pleading. Good night and my heartfelt gratitude. Elisabeth."

1921

Mercer had occasionally preached at the rural Immanuel Episcopal
Church in Glencoe, Maryland, about 18 miles north of Baltimore.
It was adjacent to the Episcopal-affiliated Oldfields School, a private school for girls. The head of the school, Rev. David McCulloch,
and his wife, Mary, had befriended Mercer and Katherine.

In March, Mercer sent Elisabeth copies of some of his sermons.
She thanked him for them on the 17th and added:

> During the last week or two, I have been feeling keenly the respon-
> sibilities of being your disciple, for God must have had some pretty
> definite idea in sending me down to Sherwood Forest to get religion.
>
> It was up to that woman of Scripture to see that Elijah had the
> best she had to give, and you must call on this woman to the limit.
> I am not thinking at all of your personal part of the fund, but how
> we (if I may say that) can best further our Big Brotherhood with
> the limited time and strength that God has given us.

While Elisabeth often served as a sort of filter through which
Mercer could pass some of his ideas, Mercer had an opportunity
to act as a filter for one of her unusual notions. On March 21, she
drafted a letter to the Episcopal Bishop of Michigan, Charles D.
Williams, known throughout the church as a strong advocate for
the Social Gospel. He also was the President of the liberal Church
League for Industrial Democracy (CLID). After identifying herself
as a member of the CLID, she asked him to consider leaving his
post in Michigan to become the Church's "Radical Bishop at Large."

She said that she and Mercer were "trustees of the One Big

Brotherhood Fund which has as its object the Kingdom on Earth of the Just One."

She said the Fund was not large,

just a few hundred dollars given each month, but if you should think it best for the good of the Church to resign from your Diocese, I think we could assure you of $2,500 a year. I know this seems a pittance but it would be something definite and I suppose that speaking and writing might bring you something!

I thought it might be of interest to you to know that there are people in Baltimore who are deeply concerned in the true Religion.

Elisabeth sent her draft to Mercer with a covering note asking him to review it and adding, "Don't think the enclosed means that I am nutty. I have had it on my mind since you spoke of Bishop Williams some months ago."

Mercer suggested it not be sent. He had written a note at the top of the draft, in pencil: "Written but not sent."

A few months later, in June, Elisabeth suggested to Mercer that he "sell a North Dakota bond" that she had given him, saying that it was her "strong desire" that he and Katherine use that bond next summer "and we three go to England. No answer is required by return mail but if you will take it under consideration, let's go slow about selling the bond."

There is no record that they ever traveled together to England, but almost immediately after making that suggestion she was making arrangements for another trip the three of them would take to a resort in Digby, Nova Scotia.

"I have decided to compromise on the OBB (One Big Brotherhood Fund). I will put in the regular sum in August but you can check on that account for traveling expenses for you and K. The board I will pay from my personal a/c."

She later asked Mercer "to do the hard work" and make arrangements for them to take a steamship from Boston to Nova Scotia. Presumably they made the trip together but there is no record of it.

On November 1, she sent him another bond and asked to keep it in his safe deposit box. She said it

> ought to be a useful thing in an emergency but use it in any way whatever if I should not be here for the book or bail! It is yours to command and no questions can be asked. When I say yours I would mean to you and Katherine.
>
> It makes me happier to leave it so, for there are sometimes awkward waits in settling estates. Yours affectionately, Elisabeth.

(Once again, perhaps because of her recent illness, or for other reasons, Elisabeth seems to convey her concern of an early death.) She thought of him on Armistice Day, November 11, 1921.

> It was a keen disappointment that you were not in the guard of honor—indeed I hoped you might be there. After all it was a beautiful finale to our overseas adventure.
>
> Would you care to have a Communion Service Sunday (presumably at 513)? Don't do it unless it appeals to you for this Anniversary. There are other times and seasons, but I have been deeply moved today. Yours and Katherine's devoted friend, Elisabeth.

Toward the end of the year, on December 3, Elisabeth wrote a poem for Mercer. The last two lines read:

Upon the Watch Tower you stand sentinel
And others light their torches from your fire.

Elisabeth Gilman with one of her pet dogs. Circa 1930. (Johns Hopkins)

Elisabeth Gilman (right) with her stepmother, Elizabeth Dwight Woolsey Gilman ("Lilly") at "Over Edge," the Gilman summer home, Northeast Harbor, Maine Early 1900s. (Johns Hopkins)

Elisabeth and her father, Daniel Coit Gilman, playing chess at "Over Edge," the family summer home at Northeast Harbor, Maine. Circa late 1890s. The home is listed on the National Register of Historic Places and is available for private rental today. (Johns Hopkins)

Mercer Green Johnston wearing his YMCA uniform and displaying the U.S. Distinguished Service Medal and the French Croix de Guerre, awarded for heroism on the battlefield in World War I. 1918. (Library of Congress)

Rev. Mercer Green Johnston (1868-1954). Late 1890s. (Library of Congress)

Katherine Aubrey Johnston passport photo circa 1917. A native of Baltimore and a graduate of Johns Hopkins School of Nursing, she and Mercer were married in 1901. She died in 1960. (Library of Congress)

Elisabeth's watercolor sketches made during a Gilman family visit to Egypt in February/March, 1890. (Johns Hopkins)

Y. M. C. A. Hotel Pavillon Paris — Writing and reading room

Wyndham, Publisher, 6 rue de Trévise

The YMCA Canteen lobby in the Hotel Pavillon at 30 rue de l'Echiquier, Paris, where Elisabeth directed programs and provided services for soldiers and sailors on rest and recreation leave from the battlefront in 1917-19. The hotel could accommodate 300-400 overnight guests. (Johns Hopkins)

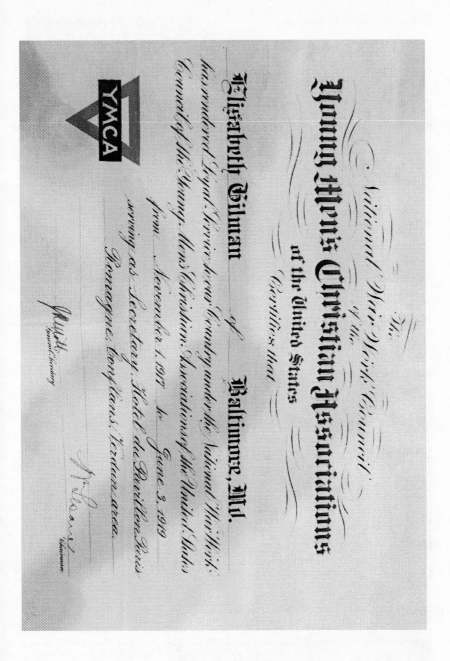

Elisabeth's "discharge" certificate following her YMCA service in France 1917-19. (Johns Hopkins)

Elisabeth Gilman (first person, front row left), in Vienna, summer, 1931, with U.S. Socialist Party Delegation to the Fourth Congress of the Second International (L.S.I.). (Johns Hopkins)

Elisabeth and chow puppies (1936). They were her favorite breed. (Johns Hopkins)

Grand SOCIALIST RALLY

FREDERICK, MD.

Sat. Night, Sept. 27, 1930
7:30 P. M.

Socialist Candidate for Governor

MISS ELIZABETH GILMAN

ELIZABETH GILMAN
Socialist Candidate for Governor

WILLIAM A. TOOLE Socialist Candidate for Attorney General

CLARENCE H. TAYLOR Member of Organized Labor

Citizens of Frederick!
Come Hear These Able Speakers.

Workers of Frederick!
Come hear the Socialist message of unemployment, and other vital issues of the campaign.

THE SOCIALIST PARTY OF MARYLAND calls upon the workers and farmers of Maryland to join with it in its purpose of securing political control of the State and Nation in order that this power might be used to put an end to the present poverty and war producing system, based upon the private ownership of the livlihood of the people, and the substitution therefore of a system based upon the collective ownership of the means of production and distribution and the democratic operation thereof, to the end that poverty, ignorance and war may be driven from our land.

The Socialist Party of Maryland declares as its solemn beleif that, with the co-operation of the labor and other moral forces of the State and Nation, it is possible to accomplish this glorious act within the lifetime of those now living; but it also declares as its solemn belief that a failure to adopt such a system will mean the destruction of civilization through the failures and iniquities of the present system and the old parties which support it.

ABSTRACT OF THE 1930 SOCIALIST PARTY PLATFORM

Campaign flyer for Elisabeth's run for Governor of Maryland on the Socialist Party ticket in 1930. Note the misspelling of her name. (Johns Hopkins)

CHAPTER 20

ELISABETH AND MERCER/1920s

For most of the early months of 1922, Elisabeth was consumed by her work on behalf of the striking miners in West Virginia. She also was touched deeply by the loss of her Aunt Louisa, who had played such a significant role in her childhood after her mother had died.

It also was a time when Mercer was working in New York for the League for Industrial Democracy at its offices at 70 Fifth Avenue in Manhattan. The League had grown out of the Intercollegiate Socialist Society that had sponsored the Sherwood Forest gathering of Socialists in the fall of 1916.

And, finally, Mercer was producing the magazine he and Elisabeth had discussed on so many occasions. It was called *The Voice of The People*.

By April 1922, it appears that for the first time since 1916 when they met, Elisabeth and Mercer were seeing less of each other and not communicating as frequently. But her affection for him and her concern for his well-being seemed as strong as ever.

Writing to him on April 5, 1922, she expressed concern that she did not know exactly where he was—New York City or Baltimore.

But, since Easter would soon be upon then, she hoped that he and Katherine could come to 513 Park Avenue for an Easter gathering.

She was moved to write another poem, which she included with that letter:

> And so your days, fighting the cause of those
> Who toil, whose danger all unheeded are,
> Are not, Oh Mercer, lost or valueless,
> Fighting their battles you have fought His foes,
> Indifference, Greed and Mammon surely box
> The way that Jesus takes the world to bless.

In November 1922, Mercer wrote a long, detailed letter to Elisabeth, saying, "we could afford to sell to the Amalgamated Clothing Workers copies of 'The Voice of the People.' It is so highly desirable to increase the circulation of the paper, I would favor being extremely liberal with the Amalgamated."

Most likely the magazine was being underwritten by the One Big Brotherhood Fund.

Christian Social Justice Fund

The most significant activity for Elisabeth and Mercer in 1923 was the creation of the Christian Social Justice Fund (CSJF), which they led. Mercer was the first president and Elisabeth was secretary for many years. Its office was at her home, 513 Park Avenue.

The CSJF had a board of trustees of prominent Baltimore business, civic, and religious leaders. Rabbi Edward I. Israel described the organization in a statement that was circulated for fund-raising purposes. The trustees, he wrote,

> meet at least once a year to dispense funds as are made annually

available by gift or bequest for the promotion of liberal and radical projects of Christian or socially religious character.

The funds are granted to educational and religious organizations whose programs are concerned primarily with economic and social reform. Legal counsel has been sought concerning exemptions of contributions to the Fund from revenue and inheritance taxes. The opinion received was that our corporation was exempt.

Elisabeth contributed generously to the Fund and, in 1925, she told CSJF trustees that she had made provision in her will for the CSJF to be the Residual Legatee "and it will receive as much as $50,000, or possibly more."

She added that the New York Socialist newspaper, *The New York Call,* and the Socialist-leaning Rand School "hold certain of my securities as collateral." She asked the board not to "embarrass" those organizations by a sudden demand for a return of the securities after her death.

As generous as Elisabeth was to the CSJF, its largest individual benefactor was William F. Cochran, the Baltimore land developer who had created Sherwood Forest, Maryland, scene of the 1916 Socialist leadership meeting. Cochran provided several thousand dollars a year to the Fund for many years.

As secretary of the CSJF, Elisabeth kept the corporate seal. On June 6, 1923, she sent Mercer a note on which she had embossed the newly acquired seal. It read: "Christian Social Justice Fund Incorporated" around the edge. In the center were two clasped hands and a shield, the phrase "whatsoever things are just," and the date of 1923.

The activities of the CSJF were always on the minds of Elisabeth and Mercer and the subject of much correspondence over many years. Cash always needed to be raised and disbursements—the amounts and the purposes—were the subjects of lengthy considerations by the Board.

1924
Early in 1924, Mercer went to Texas to be with his father, who was ill. (He would die on November 4, in San Antonio.) He had spent much of his early life in the shadow of his father, James Steptoe Johnston, a strong and colorful Civil War veteran who had become the Episcopal Church's Bishop of West Texas. Although the two men lived hundreds of miles apart, they corresponded frequently, sometimes at great length. Whenever Mercer faced worrisome issues he wrote to his father, explaining, sometimes in painful detail, the crux of the problems. His father would respond with long letters of sympathy and encouragement.

Although Elisabeth never met Bishop Johnston, the two carried on an extensive correspondence both from France and after she returned home. They became so close through the exchange of letters that, instead of signing his name, he would write "your Foster Father."

When Elisabeth learned of the seriousness of the Bishop's illness she wrote to Mercer on February 5:

It is impossible for me to tell you today of how deeply I am feeling with you. I can never forget the day I learned that the beginning of the end had come for my Father and so I realize something of what you are going through.

She concluded by reminding him that his father often had called himself her "Foster Father." She added: "As a practical matter please let me put in the enclosed."

A few days later she received from Mercer a penciled note on the letter Elisabeth had written to him: "Returning check for $150. Fraternally, MGJ."

That was an interesting response from a man who had accepted so many financial gifts from Elisabeth. Had she finally offended his pride? Was it a way of telling her he could stand on his own without her help? He may have regretted responding as he did because not long afterward he sent her a large tin of Texas pecans.

On June 16, writing to him from Alice's summer home in New Hamburg, Elisabeth told him of having attended a summer conference at Vassar College attended by "about 100 women interested in a Christian Solution to the Race Issue." She also said she soon would be "sailing from New York" on another of her European trips.

Just before she left for England, she received a letter from her cousin, Francis Gilman, executor of her Aunt Louisa's estate:

"I am sending you… a check which we believe is in accordance with what our Dear Aunt Louisa would have wished. I am only too sorry there are not more of the same sort going in the same way which I know she would have approved." There was no indication of the amount of the check.

While Elisabeth was abroad, Mercer wrote to her about his plans to attend "an important meeting in Cleveland." It probably was in connection with the formation of the Progressive Party, which took place there at that time. Elisabeth urged him to cover his expenses with funds from the One Big Brotherhood Fund. "It is yours to command," she wrote.

1925

For the first seven or eight months of this year, both Elisabeth and Mercer and Katherine were feeling ill for much of the time. In a letter written to Mercer on June 23, Elisabeth complained that she was not feeling well and was under the care of a doctor. She said she realized she had to "back off and get some rest."

She said she could be contacted through her old friend and former student tenant at 513 Park Avenue, Page Nelson, then treasurer at Johns Hopkins University.

A day later, in a letter to Mercer, she had written at the top: "At Mrs. Ames." She apparently was there to try to recuperate from whatever ailed her.

She wrote: "As K probably told you I have been pretty 'seedy' and am now trying what rest will do. I shall not leave for some days. Will phone when I have anything to say. With love to you both, E".

Mercer responded that he and Katherine also had been ill. He said they "have not been quite up to the mark; she is not sleeping well and I am bothered with a queer fuzzy feeling in my head now and have been bothered otherwise."

Whatever Elisabeth's problem may have been, she was able to throw it off and in August she visited friends in Boston, Rockport, and Northampton.

A brief note to Mercer during her trip: "Page wires me that he has deposited my JHU Annuity so I enclose the September check" (from the One Big Brotherhood Fund).

Senator Burton K. Wheeler Defense Fund

In 1924 and 1925, Elisabeth devoted large amounts of time to the so-called Wheeler Defense Fund, for which she served as treasurer.

Wheeler, LaFollette's vice presidential running mate, had been elected to the Senate in 1924 from Montana. He had been highly critical of the scandals in which high federal officials were said to be taking bribes from land development companies who wanted to develop natural resources on Federal land for their own benefit.

In his first speech on the Senate floor, Wheeler attacked Attorney

General Harry Daughtery for what he claimed was Daughtery's protection of those who profited from the infamous Teapot Dome Scandal. Daughtery was forced to resign. However, in an act of reprisal and revenge, the Justice Department, through a Federal Court in Wheeler's home state of Montana, indicted him on trumped up charges in which he was said to have illegally represented a private law client of his, for a fee, before the Department of the Interior.

The Senate almost immediately voted to exonerate him but the Montana federal court case continued until it, too, was dropped, thanks to the efforts of Elisabeth and others.

Remainder of the 1920s
During the last half of the 1920s, Elisabeth and Mercer were working harder than ever to find the necessary funds to underwrite the several causes they were supporting. They constantly were juggling money, putting gifts into one fund, withdrawing funds from another. They always seemed to be skating on financially thin ice.

Mercer was director of a lobbying organization called People's Legislative Service, in Washington. D.C. His friend, Richard Hogue, was his associate director. The mission of the PLS was described as "a non-partisan organization of citizens that supports progressive members of both houses of Congress with facts and figures and tells the people the Truth." Its efforts were closely linked to the LaFollette-Wheeler campaign and it worked to keep that movement alive.

Elisabeth used the OBB funds to reimburse the PLS for Mercer's salary throughout the years he was director.

Elisabeth, Johnston, Hogue, and Willman Cochran also were deeply engaged in managing the highly popular Open Forum.

They faced unending pressure to identify speakers, arrange for their travel to Baltimore, and make accommodations for them while they were in the city. They arranged for venues to hold the Forum's Sunday afternoon programs. And, always, they were looking for financial support over and above that which was solicited in free-will offerings at the events themselves.

Even as she was concerned about financial pressures on organizations with which she was directly associated, Elisabeth was speaking out on behalf of striking textile workers in Passaic, New Jersey. Some 15,000, nearly half of them women, were out of work in 1926-27.

In February 1927, she told Mercer she had learned that the strike was over, although not on terms she believed were fair. "A sorry settlement, but probably better not to hold out longer ... I hope I shall never again wear a piece of cloth made by them, though my dressmaker tells me it is the best."

The correspondence between Elisabeth and Mercer in 1927-28 seems almost entirely devoted to money matters. Some examples: March 27, 1927:

I have thought over what you said about the OBB and concluded that is best to have a reserve at the Mt. Vernon (bank) on which you and Katherine can draw if you need it to regain your health and if not it may come in handy...I already have posted the check of $300 to the Mount Vernon Bank. Good luck to it and to you both. You may also find it handy for your taxes which I understood you to say you meant to declare.

(Their correspondence never seems to make it precisely clear what health problems they may have had but frequently Mercer mentioned that either he or Katherine were not feeling well. Given his fragile emotional state at times and the precarious nature of their personal finances, one wonders whether each of them suffered from bouts of depression.)

From Elisabeth to Mercer, July 27, 1927, writing from a friend's cottage in Woodstock, New York:

> I wrote to Mr. Cochran…begging for funds. I enclose checks for your signature please [probably from the CSJF account]. I have used the last I have for the Pioneer Youth Camp. I suppose you have heard that an army of mosquitoes drove the Camp away from Ft. Smallwood… and now they are happily established in Anne Arundel County.

Elisabeth spent the summer of 1927 in London and France. On her return in October she picked up where she had left—worrying about finances:

Writing October 5th from New Hamburg, where she was staying with Alice, she warned Mercer that the Christian Social Justice Fund trustees probably would not be able to provide as much year-end support to his People's Legislative Service as they had done previously.

She added:

> It occurred to me as I have been thinking this over that you might be counting on these subscriptions…As I said a fortnight ago I would be perfectly willing not to sell 3420 (the Holmes Avenue property) this winter, and as I said before, if you do not want to remain tied up to the PLS for any reason, I would be delighted to go back to the old arrangement of 1926 [sending him checks from the OBB Fund]. Count on my friendship and don't hesitate to change your mind if it seems wisest.

Two weeks later:

I am fairly sure that Mr. Cochran means to cut down on his unrestricted subscriptions [to the CSJF], as well as his 'Specials,' and he already has withdrawn his promised increase of $1,000. It seems wise to pay all our pledged contributions if possible before our October board meeting so that all the Trustees can understand how we stand, especially that WFC [Cochran] should himself face the situation.

Once again, on Armistice Day, November 11, Elisabeth remembered their days together in France. She wrote to Mercer:

When I wrote the date this morning, I felt that a line of remembrance should go to you. Whatever may be our feelings against War now, certainly those were days of never-to-be-forgotten devotion.

Devotion to country? Devotion to each other? Both?
Later in November, Mercer apparently had told Elisabeth it was not necessary for her to send him a check from the OBB Fund. She replied:

It seems odd …not to be mailing you the OBB check. Are you sure [underlined] that you do not need it for this month and for the… insurance? My Hopkins quarterly annuity came today so I am on easy street, for the moment at least, so do not hesitate to let me remit as usual.

On December 12, Elisabeth wrote:

I am enclosing your Christmas present [presumably a check] with love and best of good wishes…It is the greatest pleasure to be able to do this for a much needed holiday of a good friend...

And on New Year's Eve:

Dear Mercer: The first check of the New Year [from the OBB Fund] goes to you with my constant and affectionate good wishes. You and Katherine both have suffered so much this past year, she physically and you financially, that I want your margin to be wider. You both are too valuable when manual help would lighten the burden, so this means the OBB is still extant on the old basis, for whatever you need. You...can settle...as to how much you pay the PLS for your salary.

1928

The New Year of 1928 began poorly for Mercer Johnston. As chairman of another organization, the National Progressive Headquarters, he was forced to inform NPH members that the organization's executive committee had concluded, "that a continuance of the life of this Committee would serve no worth-while purpose."

The adjournment of the Executive Committee...does not mean the end of the Progressive Movement—by no means. It still possesses elements of great strength. The power exercised by Progressives in Congress was never greater than it is at this time. Sooner or later the principles for which the Progressives fought in 1924 will assume definite militant form.

Perhaps using the Christmas gift that they had received from Elisabeth and perhaps facing physical and mental exhaustion, Katherine and Mercer went to Texas early in 1928 for a six-week vacation. When Elisabeth learned from Richard Hogue that they would be away that long, she sent a note with some cash for them. "I feel sure that you will need the enclosed, which goes with best wishes for health and strength. If you stay longer I will again remit and always with pleasure that I can be of service to you."

None of the correspondence between Mercer and Elisabeth states precisely what Mercer's health problems may have been. However, a letter he received from an Open Forum admirer may shed some light on it.

On March 11, one Charles T. Gladstone of Baltimore wrote to Mercer to say that he had "heard from Miss Gilman at the Open Forum" that Mercer would preside at the last meeting of the Forum. The announcement, he said, "was met with a good deal of applause and many expressions that you would get no more throat trouble."

In July, Elisabeth spent three weeks in Mexico. She was there when the country's president-elect, Alvaro Obregon of the Labor Party, was assassinated. On her way home, she stopped in San Antonio and went to Mercer's father's grave.

> I took some flowers out to your father's grave—to visit—it was one of the first things I wanted to do. As you know I treasure his kindness to me.

Another New Year—1929—and another difficult beginning
Mercer wrote to Elisabeth about serious dental problems: "I am trying to postpone my second battle until March but I may be unable to do so. I will let you know as soon as I know, whether it is going to be a physical impossibility for me to perform." (Elisabeth had invited him to be a speaker at Open Forum.)

In August, Elisabeth went to Europe with Alice. She wrote to

Mercer from Chamonix, France, where Mercer had scaled Mont Blanc, almost making it to the top:

> This place is so full of memories of our time here in 1918 that I must perforce, as well as by affection, write to you. This must go to your office for I cannot remember the number on Klingle Road.

Neither Elisabeth's nor Mercer's papers indicate exactly when the Johnstons moved from Holmes Avenue in Baltimore to their new home at 2015 Klingle Road, NW, in Washington, D.C. It was a house in which they would live for the remainder of their lives.

In October, Mercer reported to her again about his, and Katherine's, dental issues:

> Both K and I expect to be in for some heavy work with the dentist this month (we laid off for a while to recuperate physically and financially) and I may not be able to eat in public. A considerable part of my upstairs furniture comes out. Pity 'tis true.

Elisabeth had just returned from her European trip and sent Mercer and Katherine a note:

> I did not go in for coming-home presents this time but in a few days I shall be mailing you the throat tablets and, as I remember, Katherine's favorite brand of Paris soap, just to show you I thought of you both while there. My love goes with them.

CHAPTER 21

ELISABETH CROSSES THE "COLOR LINE"

Nothing Elisabeth did during the latter years of the 1920s attracted attention like the dinner she gave at her home in honor of the editor of *The Nation*, Oswald Garrison Villard, on March 9, 1928.

A committee of some of Baltimore's leading citizens had organized to honor the tenth anniversary of the editor of the liberal weekly. Oswald G. Villard was the son of an early publisher of *The Nation*, Henry Villard.

The committee had planned to hold a gala dinner in Villard's honor at a downtown hotel. But their plans were temporarily hampered when they learned that no hotel in Baltimore would permit its dining facilities to be used by a group that would include Negroes. The committee's invitation list had included a small number of the city's African-American population.

At first they tried to reserve a room at the Southern Hotel, the 14-story landmark hotel known as the "Queen of Light Street," and one of the best hotels in the city. A contract was set for March 9. But when the management learned that Negroes would be included among the guests, they indicated that their policy prohibited service to Negroes.

The committee tried to make reservations at other hotels in the city but each one had a policy similar to the one at The Southern.

The committee even tried to reserve the Dining Room of the Friends Meeting House on Park Avenue and Laurens Street. Surely a Quaker community would welcome them. Not so.

According to the *Baltimore Sun's* account of the issue in its March 9 edition, the committee had an agreement with the Friends group to hold the dinner in their dining room but, at the last minute, it was cancelled. "Differing explanations were forthcoming..." the *Sun* reporter wrote, "but none of them referred to 'the color line.'"

Dr. O. Edward Janney, a leader at the Meeting House, said that the action was taken "as a result of objection from the Friends School committee and from patrons of the school and did not reflect the opinion of the majority of the property committee."

A member of the property committee, Charles Blackburn, disagreed with Janney, saying the committee "was almost unanimously opposed to the use of the hall for the dinner."

One suspects that the "patrons of the school," those contributing substantial financial support, had the final say, overruling other members of the Meeting who may have been more generously inclined to make the hall available.

Whatever the facts may have been, another site had to be chosen quickly for the dinner. At that point, Elisabeth stepped into the breach and offered her home at 513 Park Avenue.

The *Sun* headline said it all: "Villard Group Loses Friends' Hall, to Dine at Gilman Home." And the sub-headline was: "Banquet in Honor of Editor To Be Held At Private House After Dispute Caused By Seating Of White And Negro Guests."

Above the headlines was a large photo of a bespectacled Elisabeth, with short hair, in a black dress with white collar, holding her favorite dog, a chow named "Claribell." (Could Elisabeth have named her dog for Baltimore's Dr. Claribell Cone? She and her sister, Etta, had collected one of the world's best known collections of modern French art.)

Two years later, *Sun* reporter Paul Ward asked her about that dinner.

"The Villard dinner cost her more socially than any of her other radical activities, Miss Gilman believes," he wrote. "But even so," she told him, "her sacrifices have not been great; the few friends she has lost have been more than made up for by the many more fascinating ones she has gained."

CHAPTER 22

ENTERING THE POLITICAL FRAY/
CAMPAIGNING FOR GOVERNOR

Elisabeth had been priming herself to enter politics for many years. Perhaps she had not planned it that way but almost everything she did, in a public way, had a political—more accurately, a Progressive—twist.

Leading the popular, well-attended Open Forum programs on Sunday afternoons at some of Baltimore largest assembly halls had placed her before hundreds of local citizens. That so many of the speakers at the Forums were identified as liberals meant that Elisabeth, by association, was seen as a reform advocate.

Also, her name was visible, regularly, in the Baltimore news columns of the *Sun*, the *American*, the *Post*, the *News* and the *Afro-American*. If they were not reporting on some social activist venture in which she was engaged, she would take the initiative and write letters to the papers to express her views on whatever might be uppermost on her mind.

Her first serious venture into political life seems to have been in the presidential campaign of 1924. Calvin Coolidge, a Republican, was the incumbent. He had been vice president but rose to the presidency after President Warren Harding died in office. The Democrats had nominated John W. Davis, a former Virginia Congressman and former Ambassador to United Kingdom. He was too conservative for many Democrats, so they split away from the party to form a third party, the Progressive Party. It was led by presidential candidate Robert M. LaFollette, a United States Senator from Wisconsin, and the vice presidential candidate, Senator Burton K. Wheeler, of Montana.

Elisabeth was an active supporter of the LaFollette-Wheeler ticket, and was selected to be a state elector for their campaign, together with the Johns Hopkins professor and social activist, Dr. Broadus Mitchell. The principles held by Progressives—federal ownership of utilities and railroads, protection of civil rights, stronger pro-labor laws for example—appealed greatly to Elisabeth and Mercer Johnston, who referred to their efforts to get LaFollette elected as "the Big Job."

"In my judgment," Mercer wrote to Elisabeth in the months leading up to the election,

> this campaign is the most important piece of work you and I have yet undertaken. It affords the best opportunity of giving practical expression to some of the fundamental things concerning society and government in which we believe, and which we believe ought to be brought down out of the realm of the theoretical into the realm of the practical.

Mercer was echoing Elisabeth's regular suggestions to him that he always should be seeking ways to convert his idealistic notions into practical applications.

Despite their efforts and to no one's surprise, Coolidge was elected and the Progressives lost the election in November 1924.

They won 16.8 percent of the national vote but only one state—LaFollette's home state of Wisconsin.

Four years later, Elisabeth was writing in the Baltimore *Post's* letters column on October 27, 1928, to urge the election of the Socialist Party's presidential candidate, Norman Thomas. She reminded her readers, "Four years ago 50,000 Progressives in Maryland voted the LaFollette-Wheeler ticket. As of today I see neither candidate of the old parties [represented by Republican President Herbert Hoover and Democrat "Al" Smith, Governor of New York] as a Progressive."

She went on to urge her fellow citizens "to help build this protest party of the future." She concluded, "Why should not we again cast a vote of 50,000 or more on the right side? Let's go to it."

Thomas had appeared in Baltimore earlier that month, on Sunday, October 7, at the Hippodrome Theater. The newspaper advertisement for that event was headlined "Come and Hear," and it included a line noting, "Elizabeth Gilman, well known Progressive, will preside." The ad had misspelled her name, a "z" instead of an "s," but she was used to that by now.

Campaign for Governor—1930: The Nomination

Less than two years after Norman Thomas, Socialist candidate for President, lost by a wide margin to Herbert Hoover in November 1928, and some seven months following the beginning of the Great Depression in October 1929, the Maryland Socialist Party called on one of its most visible, respected, and articulate members to represent the party in the gubernatorial election of 1930.

Elisabeth was their candidate. At the age of sixty-two, she became the first woman to run for the office of Governor of Maryland.

A Socialist in heart and mind since the summer of 1916, she had formally joined the Party in 1929 and had espoused its principles wherever and whenever she could assemble an audience to listen to her.

The Socialists' Nominating Convention was held in Hagerstown on May 11, 1930. In accepting the nomination, according to the *Hagerstown Morning Herald*, May 12, 1930, Elisabeth said she was gratified at the honor and she considered it given in recognition of her ten years of work in the interests of labor and for the cause of the Socialist Party.

In the race she would run against Maryland's popular sitting governor, Democrat Albert Ritchie, and the Republican candidate, Baltimore's mayor, William F. Broening. Today most Baltimoreans will recognize them for highways that bear their names.

Elisabeth never had a chance to win, and she knew it. What she wanted, and used, was a large platform—a pulpit, harkening back to her Social Gospel roots—to promote big government and corporate reform, social justice, organized labor, the needs of the retired elderly and the needy, and to condemn social and economic disasters that she believed were caused by capitalism.

Why did the Socialists choose Hagerstown as the site of their convention? Would its distance from Baltimore, 75 miles to the east, and from the state capital in Annapolis, 95 miles to the southeast, send a message to voters that the party was seeking the votes of "common people" and not those residing in the seats of political power and urbanity? Or was it because the costs of mounting a convention in Hagerstown were less than they would have been in Baltimore?

Press accounts of Elisabeth's nomination suggested that she was chosen because of her public support of Socialist candidates for president in the 1920s; her work on behalf of striking miners and railroad workers and the Ladies Garment Workers; and her outspoken advocacy for women's and Negro rights and public ownership of utilities, transportation, and natural resources.

These accounts also noted that she was well known in Baltimore for her social justice advocacy and was widely respected for her views on many subjects.

The Socialist convention opened in Hagerstown on Sunday, May 11, 1930, at the Odd Fellows Temple. That day the Party also nominated Elisabeth's running mates: William A. Toole, Baltimore, Attorney General; Charles L. Myers, Cumberland, Comptroller; and Rev. J. F. Smiley, Annapolis, Clerk of the Court of Appeals.

Prohibition was a major issue on the minds of voters and politicians at that time with strong advocates, for and against, on both sides. The Socialists, and especially Elisabeth, did not want their progressive message of reform sidetracked by a prolonged discussion of this single issue during the campaign. They passed a resolution urging that the continuation or the abolition of Prohibition be decided by referendum, preferably at the national level but, if not, at least by the individual states.

Throughout the campaign reporters and citizens asked Elisabeth for her personal position on Prohibition but she always dodged the question and urged that a referendum be held. She often was quoted as saying she did not want to have a "return to the corner saloon," suggesting she may have favored continuing Prohibition.

Another major resolution adopted by the Socialists cited the lack of adequate transportation between the state's eastern and western shores along the Chesapeake Bay. It concluded that the State should build a bridge across the bay "of such proportion that it will handle all traffic."

(There had been many calls for a Bay Bridge before and after 1930. The first span of what is now a two-span bridge was built and opened in 1952 during the administration of Governor Preston Lane. Ground was broken for it in January 1949, about two years before Elisabeth's death in December 1950.)

The platform adopted in Hagerstown, and printed in a four-page brochure, documented at length, with expressions of concern and alarm, all of the wrongs the party believed were being inflicted on the state's working-class families.

The "old parties," the Maryland Socialists believed, had policies "favorable only to the interests of big business, the railroads and bus and trolley companies, power companies, manufacturers and all other corporate entities whose greed and corruption are responsible for millions of persons being unemployed or paid unfairly low wages and who receive no old age pensions."

Failure to adopt the Socialist platform, it was said, "will mean the destruction of civilization through the failures and iniquities of the capitalist system and the two old parties that support it."

The platform, on which Elisabeth campaigned, concluded "with these following demands upon the governing forces of the state and nation"—points for action which may have seemed radical at the time, but in the years since have been substantially woven into the fabric of American society.

(A) The immediate inauguration of a system of unemployment insurance under which the unemployed worker will continue to draw a part of his pay until he is again employed.

(B) The immediate establishment of an old-age system that will guarantee the living of all persons of sixty years of age and upwards, to be given by the State or Nation as a RIGHT and not merely as a substitute for the almshouse.

(C) The establishment of a widowed mothers' pension plan.

(D) The improvement of the present workmen's compensation laws so that an injured workman will be able to draw full pay from the moment of the accident.

(E) The six-hour work day and the five-day week.

(F) The establishment of a minimum wage which will be sufficient to provide a living for an American family.

(G) The abolition of the injunction in labor disputes.

(H) The financial assistance, by the State, or the Nation, in the formation of rural cooperative farms, dairies and other rural industries.

(I) The public ownership of public utilities and natural resources.

(J) The taxation of land values.

(K) The Socialist Party stands for the referendum on the repeal of the 18th Amendment and the Volstead Act, and if repealed, demands public ownership and control of liquor by the Federal Government, and it is against the return of the saloon.

On the Campaign Trail

Immediately after Elisabeth was nominated for Governor she was flooded with telegrams and notes of congratulations from friends in Baltimore, Johns Hopkins, around the state, and across the nation.

One of the earliest came from her old friend, the Baltimore born Socialist writer and muckraker, Upton Sinclair. On a piece of stationery with a printed letterhead "UPTON SINCLAIR, Station A, Pasadena, California," he had pasted a small newspaper clipping announcing her nomination and bearing the demeaning headline: SOCIALISTS BACK GIRL IN MARYLAND.

Just below the article, in a large scrawling hand, in pencil, he wrote, "Hello Girlie." Elisabeth must have loved it. She gave it a prominent place in her scrapbook of newspaper accounts of the campaign.

She also must have been pleased to hear from Ray Newton, her former supervisor at the Pavilion Canteen in France during the war. He had helped make her life as pleasant as possible in those days and she had grown fond of him. She had often mentioned him, approvingly, in her letters to Alice and Louisa.

He wrote, on May 23, 1930, on letterhead from "The Secretarial Staff, American Friends Service Committee, 20 South Twelfth Street, Philadelphia, Pa."

"They tell me that we are going to have a woman Governor of Maryland. Congratulations! I would be delighted to help you run Maryland as I helped you run the Hotel Pavilion. I certainly hope you will poll more voters than all the other candidates put together." He signed the letter, "Ray Newton, Secretary, Peace Section."

The highly regarded Johns Hopkins physician, Dr. William H. Welch, who had been Dean of the School of Medicine and the School of Public Health, contacted her also. Despite the fact that he was supporting Governor Ritchie, he wrote to congratulate Elisabeth on her nomination. He concluded his letter:

> While I am not a Socialist, there is much in the program of your party with which I sympathize. There is a singular lack of understanding of socialist aims and policies in this country, and an unbelievable prejudice against even the name 'socialist' which would be quite incomprehensible in the countries of Western Europe today.
>
> I am, with kindest regards and all good wishes, Very Sincerely Yours, William H. Welch.

Her Baltimore friend, Felix Morley, then with the League of Nations Association of the United States as Geneva Representative, wrote on May 30 to express his "interest and surprise at the news of your nomination for Governor of Maryland Free State. If I were at home I certainly would vote for you, and feel my absence more regrettable because of a sneaking suspicion that you are going to need all the votes you can get."

In about three months Elisabeth would visit Morley in Geneva as she was making a "fact-finding" trip through Europe.

Nowhere among Elisabeth's or Mercer Johnston's papers does there seem to be any correspondence between them during this time—no notification from Elisabeth to Mercer that she intended to run for the Governor's office and no message from Mercer to Elisabeth when the announcement of her nomination became public.

CHAPTER 23

LEADING UP TO THE ELECTION FOR
GOVERNOR/1930

In June 1930, even before her nomination as Socialist candidate for Governor of Maryland was ratified, Elisabeth announced that she would go abroad to visit several European countries where socialists were active in government: Russia, England, France, Germany, and Austria.

She said the purpose of her trip was to obtain information that would give the people of Maryland a better understanding of Socialism and "something more than hot air."

After spending a few days with her sister, Alice, at her summer home in New Hamburg, New York, Elisabeth sailed from New York on June 27.

She returned to that city on September 15. Reporters met her at dockside and asked about her trip.

She expressed support and admiration for the Socialist government of Vienna and especially its public housing policies. She characterized the situation in Russia as a "magnificent experiment but one that is not needed here." She said that, "to achieve such a state of mind that exists there one must of necessity have overthrown a tyranny as existed under the Czar."

Later, she would conclude,

> I have come home with more respect for the brains of the communist
> leaders and for the social program they are attempting to carry out,
> but I am even more convinced than I was when I left the United
> States that their methods are unsuited to us. Changes here will come
> about by parliamentary action and not by violence.

In Germany, she met with two women Socialists who were
members of the Reichstag. She visited Geneva and met with offi-
cials of the League of Nations. She also saw fellow Baltimorean,
Felix Morley, who was studying the League on a Guggenheim
Fellowship and would later write a book, *The Society of Nations*.
And she dined with John Van Antwerp, head of the Walter Hines
Page School of International Relations at Johns Hopkins.

In London, Elisabeth discussed the state of Socialism in England
with the Labor Party leader, Arthur Henderson. She also visited
the Socialist, Mrs. Sidney Webb, whom she had met on her way
home from Paris in 1919. At that time she had characterized Mrs.
Webb as "rude," but on this occasion she withheld any comments
about her.

And she followed through with her plan to have vocal lessons
with the famous Viennese voice coach, Hugo Stern. She later joked
with reporters about the encounter. Saying she had taken exercises
to "develop chest notes" so her voice would have greater resonance,
she added, with a laugh, "Now I speak bass and I will have ample
opportunity to practice my new tones this fall."

While in New York she met with the Socialist leader Norman
Thomas, then a candidate for a Congressional seat, and Louis
Waldman, Socialist candidate for Governor of New York. Each

promised to come to Maryland to speak on her behalf.

Elisabeth took a train from New York to Baltimore on September 19, arriving at Mt. Royal Station at 6:30 p.m.—ready to hit the campaign trail.

Hitting the Campaign Trail

Two days later her nomination was confirmed "at a huge ratification meeting of party candidates at the Workmen's Circle Lyceum, 1029 East Baltimore Street," according to the Socialist newspaper, *The Baltimore Leader*.

That same evening, with all of Maryland's Socialist candidates present, she made the first speech of her campaign—a speech that would be followed by dozens more appearances in Baltimore and around the state over the weeks leading up to the election on November 4.

On September 27, she was featured at a rally in Frederick. It was held outdoors at West Second and Court Streets, opposite the county courthouse. Two others also spoke: Rev. Clarence Whitmore, who stood in for Attorney General candidate William Toole, and Clarence Taylor, a Baltimore labor leader who introduced Elisabeth.

In advance of the event, Maryland Socialists had produced hundreds of flyers—headlined "Grand Socialist Rally"—listing the speakers and this invitation:

> Citizens of Frederick! Come Hear These Able Speakers.
> Workers of Frederick! Come hear the Socialist message of unemployment and other vital issues of the campaign.

A photo of Elisabeth was featured prominently on the flyer. She is seen smiling slightly, wearing a black dress and pince-nez glasses on the bridge of her nose.

The *Frederick News* described the crowd at the 7:30 p.m. meeting as "a small audience." But the Party's paper, the *Maryland Leader*, reported that, "several hundred people turned out to greet the first woman candidate for Governor of the State."

Elisabeth opened her talk by describing what she saw as the distinctions between communism and socialism.

She said she wanted to make it clear that there was a fundamental difference between the two and she believed that many people did not understand that difference. Communists, she said, seek by violent means a coup d'état to overthrow the government of a country and substitute a dictatorship of the proletariat, while Socialists seek their ends through the ballot.

> The Socialist Party wishes to make the world a better place for everyone to live in and as a means toward this end it advocates public ownership and administration of basic industries, especially that of electric power.

She concluded:

> Voters need not feel that they are losing their vote if they should not elect the Socialist candidates this year because this is an educational campaign and the foundation is being laid for the future when the farmer and laborer will come into their own.

In October, Elisabeth returned to Hagerstown, then on to Frostburg and Cumberland and back to Baltimore. And so it went up until the election.

The subjects of her speeches were drawn from the Party's Hagerstown platform and sometimes focused on specific topics such as "Social Insurance, the Workers' Security," or "What the Socialist Party Means to the Worker."

As often as possible, she tried to portray Governor Albert C. Ritchie as a pawn of Maryland's big businesses and industries. She also took aim at the Governor's "Ritchie Citizenship League," comprised of supporters whom Elisabeth believed operated against the best interests of the state's working people.

Among the people she cited were those "high up" in the management of Baltimore Trust Co., the U.S.F. & G, Equitable Trust Co., the Arundel Corp., Fidelity Trust Co, the Safe Deposit & Trust Co., the First National Bank, Drovers and Mechanics Bank, and others.

Sadly for Elisabeth, several of her old Johns Hopkins friends were on the Ritchie team, including her dear friend, Joseph S. Ames, then president of Johns Hopkins University, along with several prominent professors at the Johns Hopkins School of Medicine and leading alumni.

Mayor William F. Broening did not escape her barbed comments. Elisabeth always owned one or two pet dogs. Often she was seen walking with them, and they appeared in newspaper pictures with her. She took advantage of a headline-grabbing dispute between Broening and the Baltimore SPCA to suggest that he "lacked empathy and human kindness for animals."

On October 17, Elisabeth made history by being the first Socialist candidate for public office to speak in the Maryland House of Delegates at Annapolis.

Two days later she was host at her home at 513 Park Avenue to a group of about 75 friends and supporters at a reception in honor of Morris Hillquit, chairman of the Socialist Party of America, who had come to Baltimore to speak on her behalf. Hillquit stayed at her home while in Baltimore.

In those years, political parties often tried to attract audiences to their rallies by offering entertainment.

Before Hillquit spoke at a rally for Elisabeth, at the Auditorium Theater, musicians from the Baltimore Symphony Orchestra, led by Jacob Turk, concertmaster, presented a mini concert.

In his talk before 1,200 people, Hillquit blamed Republicans and Democrats and their supporters in business and industry for creating the Great Depression. He called for reduced working hours, pensions for retired workers, unemployment insurance, the cancellation of World War I Allied war debts, and disarmament.

In the days just before the November 4 election, Elisabeth was speaking at least once a day, sometimes three times, to audiences in Baltimore.

On November 2, she spoke at three separate sites. In the afternoon, at 3:30 p.m., she was at the Pride of Baltimore Elks' Hall, 1112 Madison Avenue, to address an African-American audience.

On the Elks Hall platform with her that afternoon was Frank M. Crosswaite, a well-known African-American labor leader, who was a Socialist candidate for Congress from New York. Early in his career he had been an organizer for the fledgling Brotherhood of Sleeping Car Porters and, after that, was closely affiliated with A. Philip Randolph, the highly respected head of that union.

Later, at 8 p.m. she appeared before Baltimore's Theosophical Society at the organization's Lodge at 523 North Charles Street. It must have been a brief appearance because, shortly after that, she spoke at the Amalgamated Clothing Workers' Hall, at 107 North Eutaw Street.

A former Baltimorean, identified in the *Sun* as "a former conservative turned Socialist labor leader," was the principal speaker at the clothing workers' meeting hall. He was Charles W. Ervin, of Chicago, a senior union organizer. He had returned to Baltimore, at Elisabeth's request, to help boost her campaign.

Ervin recognized that Elisabeth had little chance to win but, he concluded, "In the words of the late Eugene V. Debs, 'Isn't it better to vote for what you want, even if you don't get it, than to vote for what you don't want, and get it?'"

Elisabeth's remarks at the Elks' Hall were reported in Baltimore's *Afro-American* newspaper. She had focused on conditions at the State Penitentiary in Baltimore. Despite Governor Ritchie's claims that a recent survey gave high marks to the prison, Elisabeth said, "morale is poor and the plant one of the worst in the east."

Earlier that day the *Afro-American*, in an editorial, had wondered how Black women across the state would react to Elisabeth's candidacy.

Just how many Negro women in Maryland will cast their votes for Miss Elisabeth Gilman, running on the Socialist ticket for governor, will be interesting to notice, the paper said.

A number of Negro women, like their white sisters, have gone in for politics with the same appetite for the loaves and the fishes as the male of the species, but we are still simple enough to believe that the great bulk of them, if they are interested enough to vote at all, still will be guided by their instinctive attitude towards the best interests of the community.

Miss Gilman, known for her liberal attitude towards public questions affecting the Negro group, would afford an excellent opportunity for the exercise of this instinct among women voters.

The Gilman for Governor Campaign concluded with much fanfare on the evening of November 3, 1930.

It began with an open-air rally at the corner of Broadway and Baltimore Street. That was preceded by what the *Sun* described as a "torchlight automobile procession starting from the War Memorial

Plaza at 7:30 and which wound through the streets of the north-
eastern and eastern sections of the city."

The *Baltimore Post* reported "a large crowd" was present for the
rally to hear Elisabeth's final plea for their votes. Other Socialist
candidates also spoke.

The next evening, November 4, Elisabeth and her fellow candidates and friends gathered at the Party's headquarters on East
Baltimore Street to await the election returns. They were, the *Post*
reported, "confident that the Socialist Party will poll the largest
number of votes ever received in Maryland."

Maryland Leader, the state's Socialist newspaper, placed a large
box on its front page urging all Socialists to join together to mon-
itor the returns.

> COME HEAR THE SOCIALIST ELECTION RETURNS, [the ad
> read].
>   All Socialists and their friends will be there.
>   All Socialist election returns, local and national, will be received
> here.
>   Beginning at 9 P.M. until_____
>   Moving pictures will be shown
>   We will all have a good time—at the Workmen's Circle Lyceum,
> 1029 East Baltimore Street.
>   Come and bring your friends.

The Aftermath

The loyal Socialists who gathered on that November 4th evening
in East Baltimore never dreamed they could win the election—not
Elisabeth, nor any of Maryland's Socialist candidates. But after all
the returns were in, their spirits were lifted up by the fact that 4,178
Marylanders had given her their vote. That was almost twice as

many as the Socialist candidate for Governor had received four years earlier.

Elisabeth, always the realist, perhaps uncomfortable among those party members who enjoyed post-election celebrations, slipped away and headed for the late train to New York. She said she had a speaking engagement in the city the next day, although there is no record of such an event among her papers.

She stayed at Manhattan's upscale Cosmopolitan Club, at Lexington Avenue and 40th Street. It was there, the next morning, about 7:30 am, that she began to receive Western Union telegrams from Party headquarters in Baltimore giving her up-to-date returns.

A month later William E. Bohn, editor of New York's Socialist newspaper, the *New Leader*, wrote to congratulate Elisabeth. On the letterhead of Socialist-oriented Rand School of Social Science in New York, he wrote on December 8:

> Nathan Fine is in the act of computing the Socialist vote in the last election. He has just shouted over the transom that you got more than four thousand, an increase of more than one hundred fifty percent...I am writing to congratulate you. Maryland is naturally a difficult state for us. The run which you made seems to indicate that we have at last made a real impression.

A year later, on November 4, 1931, Baltimore's *Evening Sun* printed an article written by Gustav Bisgyer, titled "An All-Maryland Eleven." In it Bisgyer used the notion of an "All American Football Eleven to select a group of individuals who actually have made contributions to Maryland's welfare."

Elisabeth made the *Sun*'s team, along with her gubernatorial rival Albert Ritchie, two former mayors of Baltimore and two old Hopkins friends, Drs. William Welch and William H. Wilmer. She was listed at number 10, just ahead of Baltimore's iconic newspaperman H.L. Mencken.

In his comments about her, Bisgyer said: "You may not agree with everything Elisabeth says, but you admire her courage and her intelligent viewpoints on all subjects. Her work with the Open Forum is alone worthy of her name being listed in this group."

As demanding as a political campaign can be on a candidate, as physically tiring, as frustrating, Elisabeth must have enjoyed enough of the rewards of running for office that she became the perennial Socialist candidate for different statewide and Baltimore elections over the next dozen years.

She ran for United States Senator (1934 and 1938), Mayor of Baltimore (1935), even Sheriff of Baltimore (1942), and, one last time, for Governor, in 1945. In each race, she received little voter support. But each venture into the political fray gave her one more opportunity to give the people of her city and state her views about what Socialism stood for and why it should be important to them.

And, privately, each one of those campaigns—aimed at developing policies that would help working men, women, and their families to live healthy, productive lives—gave her another opportunity to satisfy her life-long desire to advance the Kingdom of God on Earth.

CHAPTER 24

CONFLICT BETWEEN MERCER AND ELISABETH

The onset of the Great Depression at the end of 1929 filled the early months of 1930 with fears of doom and gloom. And though 1930 became an exceedingly important and positive year for Elisabeth—the year she would campaign for governor of Maryland as the nominee of the Socialist Party—it also was a year in which her relations with Mercer Johnston became strained and uncomfortable.

Support for the People's Legislative Service (PLS), which he directed in Washington, had almost vanished as most of his donors conserved what financial resources they had. He was desperate to obtain funds for the PLS from the Christian Social Justice Fund (CSJF), which he and Elisabeth had launched in 1923 to fund "educational and religious organizations whose programs are concerned primarily with economic and social reform." A key donor to the Fund had been William Cochran, but by the late 1920s his financial support had begun to wane.

Elisabeth had warned Mercer for several years that the CSJF was in a financial bind. She had suggested that it might not be possible for it to support the PLS as generously as before. But it soon would become clear that he did not want to receive that kind of news.

In the spring of 1930, Mercer, who had been the first president of the CSJF, wrote to the Fund's trustees with a plea for funds for the PLS:

Dear Friends—At the close of perhaps the most important and useful year of its existence, the People's Legislative Service is face to face with a financial crisis that threatens its life.

To enable it to meet this crisis, and to carry through, at least to the end of the current year, work of great public importance it has in hand, application is hereby made for an appropriation of $1,000 out of the Special Fund of the CSJF in addition to the renewal of the appropriation of $500 a year which the Service has been enjoying.

In addition, he said, he normally would need $25,000 a year to run the PLS but he would reduce that, in the year ahead, to $15,000. He said he had a monthly payroll for six people costing about $925 and there were other expenses of rent, supplies, etc.

He concluded: "With great appreciation for past generous treatment and trusting that this appeal will strike home to the heads and hearts of the Trustees, I am Very Sincerely Yours."

The trustees met on May 9, 1930.

They had received proposals from 35 organizations seeking CSJF support. In addition to the PLS, they included such organizations as the Church League for Industrial Democracy; Committee on Militarism in Education; Fellowship for Reconciliation (work in Latin America); NAACP; Peace Section of Friends Service Commission; Religion and Labor Bureau; the Rand School of Social Science; and a Summer School for Women in Industry.

The Open Forum had an application for support, as did Antioch College, which said it was seeking funds for the salary of its chaplain, Paul Jones. Jones had been the Episcopal Bishop of Utah. He was a Socialist and pacifist. When he opposed the United States' entry into World War I, he was forced to leave the church. He spent the rest of his life advocating for civil rights, social reform, and economic justice.

Taking note of their own poor financial position, the trustees voted to decline or postpone action on most of the proposals.

Despite the fact that Mercer was present at the meeting the trustees voted to approve only a portion of his request. Elisabeth, the secretary/treasurer, was given the task of communicating for-mally with Mercer, which she did on May 12:

> Dear Mercer: The first check of our new financial budget goes to the People's Legislative Service—$250 which is the balance of last October's pledge and the $500 voted last Friday, $750 in all. I am glad that you do not need more at the moment and personally I feel assured that in October the other $500 will be sent. As we only have Mr. Cochran's check for $5,000 and a balance of about $2,300, we will have to divide the applications already made.

She added that she was sorry there was not more time to hear about the work of the PLS.

> Personally I have felt that I know very little of what is being done. Assuredly all Trustees have a high regard for you and what you have done, and if we erred in being very business-like, I think it was due to our desire to make every grant impartially and without personal feelings towards any person making a request.

Mercer was furious. He responded a week later, acknowledging receipt of the $750, and then, bristling with sarcasm: "Receipts for

the same are enclosed. They go, as they say, 'with our sincere thanks.'"
There was much more:

I am still not in a mood to talk much about the meeting on May
9th. There were phases of it that recalled my last vestry meeting in
Newark. The parable of the tares and the wheat has come to have
new meaning to me. Perhaps you will realize how unprepared I was
for the plan, apparently at least partially prearranged and discussed,
to throw a stone instead of a lifesaver to my organization, when I
tell you that I talked frankly with Mr. Cochran of the situation that
confronts me, in my office, in the presence of Mr. Hogue, and that
several days later…he sent this message to M. Hogue: "Tell Mercer
I read with great interest the other morning the latest bulletin of
the People's Legislative Service. I felt very clearly that it was most
worthwhile. I hope the Trustees of the Fund will feel kindly disposed
toward helping it in so far as they can in keeping it alive."

Of course something happened after this which is responsible for
the change that came over the spirit of his dream. Somebody—presumably you—for some strange reason, evidently persuaded him
against his kindlier personal judgment, that it would be better to lent
in the 'striking off' of the organization (to which I was singularly
devoted, and which has an unequaled record of public service here
in Washington, and, I think, an unequaled reputation) than to lend
a hand in 'keeping it alive.'

He signed the letter with a large, scrawled, "Mercer."
Elisabeth replied immediately:

When Mr. Cochran tells us whether he plans to make any deposit
of his subscription between now and June 1 and October 1, I will
let you know.

I believe Mr. Cochran means to write to you himself so I will not take up the points you make about the meeting, for in my letter of May 12, I wrote quite frankly. Yours Sincerely, Elisabeth Gilman.

Not satisfied to protest to Elisabeth alone, Mercer also wrote to her cousin, George Gilman, who was a member of the CSJF board.

He said he "was completely taken off my guard by the attitude of my friend, Billy Cochran (who during the sixteen years of our acquaintance had never manifested towards me anything but the sweetest friendliness accompanied by a generous consideration of whatever I was interested in)."

There were more letters from Mercer to George Gilman despite the fact that Gilman, each time he responded, tried to assure Mercer that the trustees would continue to support the PLS.

Perhaps he realized that he had overreacted to the action of the trustees.

On May 26, Mercer thanked Elisabeth again for the $750. "It adds to the sense of gratitude, of which my heart is full, for the appropriation itself which is of fundamental importance.

It pleases me very much to know of your pleasure in sending the check. Billy (Cochran) was kind enough to tell me that he was much pleased over the vote to make the appropriation. I find such satisfaction in my work as director that nothing appeals to me more these days than the willingness of my friends to see the work through my eyes as well as their own.

But then Mercer could not resist adding this to his letter:

The only appropriation in which he [Cochran] said his judgment quite decidedly did not go along, was the one for the West Virginia

miners. You are more or less familiar with his views as to appropria-
tions for strike relief and kindred causes. He said he thought to vote
anything like $1,500 to work of this unfruitful kind in one year did
not show good judgment. Of course he was speaking confidentially,
but I venture to pass this on as far as you. Yours Sincerely.

Although there is no indication that Elisabeth sent a written
reply to Mercer, his insensitive, unkind remarks about a cause to
which she had given so much of herself must have hurt.

Perhaps because funds had become so scarce, or simply because
Elisabeth and the CSJF trustees wanted to become better stew-
ards of the funds entrusted to them, she wrote to the board on
Christmas Eve 1930.

She discussed several matters under board consideration and
then concluded:

> Another matter that I wish to bring before you is what standard
> we should require from those making requests for grants. Should
> we in all cases ask for a financial statement, should we ask if they
> could do better work if a comparatively large grant were given at
> one time or whether they prefer a smaller grant every year? What
> other suggestions would you make along these lines?

Two weeks later Mercer, not surprisingly, expressed the opposite
point of view:

> My feeling is that, on the whole, the somewhat informal way in
> which we have reached our decisions has been a rather good way.
> These conclusions have been better, in my judgment, for not being
> the result of rigid rules. Whether I am exceptional in this matter,
> I do not know, but narrow definitions of what can be done and

what cannot be done, hard and fast rules as to method, do affect me unpleasantly. In a word, I suggest that we go along much as we have been doing, avoiding rigidity as much as possible.

A few days later, on January 28, the trustees disregarded Mercer's point of view and voted to establish guidelines for organizations seeking funds from the CSJF.

At their April 6, 1931, meeting the trustees "voted unanimously to send $1,500 to the West Virginia miners."

Elisabeth knew how difficult it was for Mercer to accept these two board actions. In a handwritten note headed "Good Friday night" she wrote:

On this day of better human relations, I like to keep my friendships in good repair. Apparently there have been some misunderstandings, which is beyond my understanding, but I want you to know that you and Katherine are always remembered in my prayers and that you can be assured of my friendly feelings. Yours sincerely, Elisabeth Gilman

He replied a few days later: "Thank you for your friendly note of Good Friday. I would have replied to it right away but I have gone from day to day expecting to make a trip to Baltimore to get a prescription for new glasses, at which time I expected to see you."

Mercer planned to attend the next CSJF meeting, which would be held at Cochran's home and Elisabeth invited him to spend the night at 513 Park Avenue. "I don't know quite how many I shall put up, but I know you will not mind the informality of a bed in a study, should everyone else turn up."

If he replied, there is no record of it.

CHAPTER 25

DECLINE OF THE SOCIALIST PARTY
IN THE UNITED STATES

It would be hard to imagine that Elisabeth did not understand where the Socialist Party stood in the minds of American voters when she entered the race for Maryland's Governor in 1930.

Six years earlier, in the election of 1924, she had supported, and was an elector for, Wisconsin's former Governor and U.S. Senator, Robert "Fighting Bob" LaFollette, who ran for president as a member of the Progressive Party, which he had founded. The Socialist Party, labor organizations, and others were among his strongest supporters.

LaFollette carried his own state and 17 percent of the national vote—a very good showing for a third party but not a serious challenge to the Democrats and Republicans.

But as Socialists looked back upon their decision to cooperate with LaFollette's Progressive Party in the 1924 election, they decided that it had been a mistake and that independence, with no affiliations with any other party, should be a fundamental position of the Party.

They struck out on that course and fared even more poorly in the years ahead.

In 1928, Norman Thomas was the Party's candidate for president. He was beaten badly by Herbert Hoover, who took more than 58 percent of the vote. Democrat Al Smith received almost 41 percent and Thomas was a distant third—at about three-quarters of 1 percent.

Most astute followers of politics would have seen Thomas's dramatic loss as a clear sign that the Socialists were in trouble. But if Elisabeth had followed the history of the Party, she would have known that its decline had begun to unfold much earlier.

Consider the following negative trends as presented in James Weinstein's 1967 publication, "The Decline of Socialism in America 1912-1925."

Weinstein said the Party's popularity, measured by its strength in elections, peaked in 1912 when Eugene V. Debs polled 6 percent of the national vote, an achievement never exceeded again. Also, in that year, some 1,200 Socialists held public office in states and municipalities across the country, including seventy-nine mayors in twenty-four states.

In 1912 there were more than 300 Socialist newspapers and magazines, published in English and foreign languages.

The Milwaukee Leader had a daily circulation of 35,000. It has been reported that total circulation of the Socialist press in these years may have exceeded 2 million. The mission of the Socialist media was to educate readers about the principles of socialism and to drum into their consciences the evils of capitalism.

Socialists were doing well until the United States entered World War I. War hysteria, and a fear of dangerous "un-American radicals" who opposed the nation's entry into war, as many believed Socialists to be, prompted the federal government to clamp down on the Socialist press. For example, the second-class mail privileges the papers had enjoyed were revoked under policies of the Espionage Act of 1917.

While most Socialists opposed the war, some, like Elisabeth and Mercer Johnston, did not. Although there is no evidence that Elisabeth had spoken publicly in favor of the nation sending troops to Europe, Johnston had done so frequently.

In April 1917, the Socialists met in a national "emergency meeting" to formulate a position on the war. They scheduled the meeting for April 7.

Congress had declared war on Germany the day before, on April 6.

They adopted a resolution that called the declaration of war "a crime against the people of the United States" and urged solidarity among the working-class people of the world.

The split between the pro-war faction and the anti-war proponents had weakened party unity. In addition, the pacifists became the target of hostility and violence from local, state, and federal officials and vigilante groups. In July 1917, some 8,000 Socialists and trade unionists marched for peace in Boston and were attacked by organized groups of soldiers and sailors. Boston's Socialist headquarters was ransacked.

Despite incidents like this, Socialists made a good showing in municipal elections in 1917-18, probably because many Americans sided with their anti-war position.

Morris Hillquit came in third in a four-man race for Mayor of New York in September 1917. That was good enough for the *New York Evening Post* to comment: "The Socialists have won admission, as it were, to the family of political parties."

The beginning of the Great Depression in 1929 provided the Socialists with new opportunities to reach out to their traditional base of working-class citizens and the party got a temporary lift by the mass discontent that had spread across the country.

In the 1932 presidential elections, won handily by Franklin D. Roosevelt, Socialist candidate Norman Thomas received about 900,000 votes, 2.5 percent of the national total. Party newspaper circulation rebounded from 300,000 in 1928 to 700,000 in 1932, and there was strong electoral support for Socialists in cities like Milwaukee, Reading, Bridgeport, and New York City.

A major problem for the Socialists after 1932 was Franklin Roosevelt's New Deal programs. On issue after issue, Roosevelt was proposing one social welfare program after another and Congress was putting them into law. Many touched on the same issues the Socialists had addressed in their party's platform years earlier. Roosevelt had co-opted the Socialists. Many joined his administration, further weakening the central party.

It was in this political environment, in the 1930s, that Elisabeth was seeking public office. She was not in the vanguard of a particularly popular cause. Why did she choose to keep campaigning for public office?

She probably shared Eugene Debs' view that she had a duty to educate the public about the virtues of socialism.

Socialist propaganda, Socialist electioneering, Socialist rhetoric were not merely used as bait to obtain votes but were a means to educate the public, especially working-class citizens, in the hope that they would develop a deep and abiding Socialist consciousness.

As Elisabeth had said earlier, her commitment to Socialism was a religious calling as much as a political one. She, like Vida Scudder, saw a clear link between the ideals of Socialism and the imperatives of the Social Gospel. Running for office enabled her to carry out her commitment to advance the Social Gospel.

So, while the Socialist Party may have been in decline, Elisabeth took advantage of the great affection in which she was held by many in Maryland—and especially the media—to campaign for a cause in which she so fervently believed.

CHAPTER 26

CAMPAIGNS AND OTHER ACTIVITIES AFTER
1930 ELECTION

The 1930 gubernatorial campaign seemed to have energized Elisabeth. If there were a public protest about some issue close to her heart, she would be there, to join or even lead it. Elisabeth Gilman, at sixty-three, was one of Baltimore's most visible and engaged citizens. She made for "good copy," and writers and editors gave her plenty of space on their pages.

In this post-campaign, post-election period, she was, as she often liked to say, "getting at the root of things." And she attracted almost as much media attention—perhaps more—than she had during the campaign.

On December 15, 1930, the *Evening Sun* reported that Elisabeth joined a delegation of labor leaders, led by Socialist Norman Thomas, who traveled to Washington, D.C., to press Congress for a $500,000 relief fund for unemployed workers. They visited several Congressional leaders, reminding them that seventeen million people were unemployed and urging them to provide immediate assistance.

That same month there was a labor crisis in Danville, Virginia.

Some 4,000 cotton mill workers were in the midst of a twelve-week strike. Their union, the Textile Workers of America, was beginning to run out of funds to support them. Food and clothing were in short supply. Strikers were forced to chop down trees for firewood to heat their homes. Many of the men doing this work did not have safe and durable shoes.

Elisabeth solicited friends for money to buy shoes for them. As chair of the Socialist Committee for Danville Relief, she traveled to Danville, just before Christmas, to take clothing to the striking workers and Christmas presents for their children.

She also provided "Funds to Feed Cows of Danville Strikers," according to an article in the *Baltimore Sun*. The paper reported that Elisabeth had collected $83 from her friends, and sent it to the workers' union with instructions to buy feed for the workers' communal dairy herd. The cows were needed, she said, to supply milk for more than 7,000 children living in that area.

In Baltimore, Elisabeth lobbied city officials to do more to assist the unemployed. So many families were in need of food that Elisabeth feared outbreaks of starvation in the city. In an open letter to Mayor Howard W. Jackson, she urged him to tell the public what plans he had to deal with this issue. If he had no plans, she said, "starvation and riots" would follow.

Representatives of Associated Jewish Charities, Catholic Charities, and the Family Welfare Fund supported Elisabeth's efforts and said they were serving thousands of needy families, but their funds would be exhausted within four months.

In November 1931, the *Baltimore Sun* reported that Elisabeth would take part in an Anti-Fascist rally in Washington, D.C., to protest the arrival there of the Italian Foreign Minister, Dino Grandi. She tried to play down her involvement. She told the *Sun* that while she "naturally is opposed to Fascism," she knew of no plans for a protest. She did, however, join with others in signing an anti-Fascist document protesting his presence in the country.

Perhaps her reluctance to be seen as a leader in any protest against Grandi lay in the fact that the Foreign Minister and his wife would be visiting two prominent Baltimoreans, John Work Garrett and his wife, Alice, at Evergreen, their North Charles Street mansion in Baltimore. Garrett, an influential Johns Hopkins trustee, and his wife, undoubtedly became acquainted with Grandi when Garrett was the U.S. Ambassador to Italy between 1929 and 1933. Garrett later would bequeath the Evergreen property to the university. Today it is a university house museum and rare book library.

On occasion, Elisabeth would prod her Democratic opponent in the 1930 gubernatorial campaign. In a March 1932 letter to Governor Ritchie, she urged him to give the public his views on unemployment insurance.

"Unless you take an intelligent and strong stand," she wrote, "for both the short-range and long range help for unemployment, we fear it might be said of you as it has been said of President Hoover—billions for bankers but not a dollar for the starving unemployed."

Ritchie responded on March 26, saying he believed it was "the duty of the Federal Government to collect facts on unemployment, but I have made no direct request of the Federal Government to do so."

He said further, "It never occurred to me that those in authority felt the need of any direct advice from me." He added, "It is hardly the province of the Governor of the State to undertake, as you suggest, 'to bring pressure' on members of the Senate to pass legislation." A rather astonishing statement when one considers the actions of contemporary governors who seek support for their states from the federal government.

Ritchie may temporarily have worn down Elisabeth. On April 1, she thanked him for his comments and said, "I think it is unnecessary to further discuss at present Unemployment Relief, although I do feel that, as Governor of Maryland, you are unduly modest in withholding your recommendation to the Federal Government urging the collection of facts in this nationwide question."

In May, Elisabeth traveled to Milwaukee for the Socialist Party's National Convention, where the Party nominated Norman Thomas to run as its candidate for President in November 1932.

Elisabeth joined his campaign. The *Sun*, on September 11, 1932, reported that she had "returned to Baltimore yesterday" having spent the summer in Europe and "left almost immediately for Western Maryland, where she plans to spend the next ten days" campaigning for Norman Thomas. The tour was sponsored by the Johns Hopkins Thomas-for-President Club and featured a red fire truck called "The Red Special."

As soon as she returned to Baltimore, she protested poor working conditions in the city's needle trades industry. The women in the city's male-dominated clothing industry were striking for higher wages and improved working conditions. Elisabeth had organized a group of prominent women to discuss the issue at a meeting in downtown Baltimore at the YWCA.

Elisabeth and Elinor Pancoast, an economics professor at Goucher College, who was secretary of the group, urged Baltimoreans to "acquaint themselves with the issues at stake and lend their support to a just settlement of the strike."

CHAPTER 27

"AN ABSOLUTE PACIFIST"

B y the early 1930s Elisabeth's stance on pacifism had evolved
dramatically.

Earlier, when the United States went to war in Europe in 1917,
many, if not most, of the national leaders of the Socialist Party
were strongly opposed. Elisabeth was not.

Correspondence and records of her activities in the months
just before the United States entered the conflict suggest that her
decision to support the war effort was made quickly, without a
lot of thought.

Most likely her views about the war, and United States involvement in it, were greatly influenced by Mercer Johnston. He had
made such a positive impression on her at the Sherwood Forest
Socialist conference in the summer of 1916 that one can believe
that he, more than anyone else, convinced her to "sign up," with
him and his wife, Katherine, for service in France.

But when Elisabeth came home from France in 1919, her views
had changed. When did they change? Not once, in any of her
letters to Alice or Aunt Louisa, did she ever suggest she would
become a pacifist.

Yes, she wrote about hardship, about deaths of soldiers, some of whom she knew, and she lamented the atrocities committed by the German army—atrocities that she had heard about from refugees. Yet she never said she was opposed to war as a matter of principle.

Following the War in France most Protestant denominations spoke out in opposition to war. Even the YMCA fostered pacifism. More than 100 peace groups were organized in the 1920s. It seems clear that Elisabeth's post-war views harmonized with these movements.

By 1933, she had clearly embraced the pacifist cause. On April 11 of that year, she wrote a brief statement explaining her journey toward pacifism. It was headed "Multinational Disarmament," and seemed intended for publication or perhaps for use in a speech. It is in one of her scrapbooks in the Johns Hopkins Hamburger Archives.

Excerpts:

Fifteen years ago today I was working in Paris at a canteen for the enlisted men of our army and navy. I felt that I was doing my bit to help win the War—the war to end war.

I can remember saying to a group of soldier boys, 'Oh no, I'm not one of those damn pacifists.'

I was not greatly appalled by the horror of war—though Zeppelin bombs were coming down on us in Paris killing innocent victims, though the Big Guns many miles away brought desolation to many about me, though I saw the boys go out one night never to return. For I still believed in war.

Fifteen years have gone by and I am now an absolute pacifist. I am a War Resister, pledged to take no part in any war, not in canteen or Red Cross work, not by purchase of Liberty Bonds.

Why this change in me and many thousands of others? As I see it, the absolute futility of war to give real protection to a country makes preparedness for war an outrage against civilization.

…we organize a war on account of fear of attack…of interference with our projects…that we will not maintain our place in the sun, that our financial investments abroad will not be safeguarded. I maintain that this position is illogical and absolutely futile.

Must we not decide to fight against war preparedness, against war itself? Einstein said that if two percent of the people of the world would take the absolute position that they would not take part or encourage any war, there would be no more war. It is a challenge to moral courage.

She returned to this subject again, in September 1933, when she delivered a stirring speech on non-violence in Chicago at an international conference of The Fellowship of Faith.

It behooves us to ask ourselves and to answer honestly whether we have been led by our religious faith truly to work for a peaceful method of settling disputes which make for the betterment of all mankind.

Again, I speak as an American looking back on the World War in which as a Socialist I deeply regret that I played my part in France, but did not all churches and most synagogues support the war and join in its propaganda?

Here and there were prophets of a better way…but they were the exception and not the rule.

She concluded with two quotations.
The first derived from what she called "the motto of Shintoism."

All men who dwell under heaven

Regard all beings as your brothers and sisters
You will then enjoy this divine country
Free from Hate and Sorrow.

Then she offered an excerpt from a speech given by Eugene V.
Debs in 1917.

Comrades the time will come
In this and every nation when we humanize humanity
And civilize civilization.

In 1934, the *Sunday Sun* published a photographic series called
"The First World War." It depicted the harsh realities of that war
through pictures made during the fighting in France. A full-page
letter from Elisabeth, complete with a formal photo of her, accompanied the feature.

She commended the *Sun* for the publication and continued:

As one who was in France from August, 1917, to May, 1919, I can
testify to the vividness of these photographs.

Had there been such portrayal of a former war, it is possible that
I, too, would have been convinced of the futility of settling international differences by the appeal to arms, but I did not know what war
was and the war hysteria influenced me as it did millions of others.

I only hope that the photographs…will make the younger people
more steadfast in their high resolve not to fight in behalf of any
king or country.

CHAPTER 28

ADVOCATING FOR CAUSES/1930s - 1940s

Throughout the 1930s and into the early part of the 1940s, Elisabeth rallied to support a large variety of important causes, from anti-lynching efforts to the Workers' Defense League.

Anti-Lynching Efforts

Elisabeth's unbounded support for the rights of minorities was well known in Baltimore and among others, nationally, who shared her belief that the protection of civil rights was fundamental to a democracy.

For many years, especially in Southern states, black men who were believed to have committed crimes against whites were kidnapped by mobs and lynched. Often these gruesome events were witnessed by large groups of local citizens who would cheer on the mob and, sometimes, attack the victim themselves, whether he was still living or dead.

In the United States, between 1882 and 1964, nearly 5,000 people, mostly African-American men, were killed by lynching.

In 1894, the House of Representatives called for an investigation of lynching, but it went nowhere. In 1922, the House passed a bill making lynching a federal crime. It had President Warren Harding's support but Southern senators filibustered it and it failed.

After the election of President Franklin D. Roosevelt in 1932, his supporters had high hopes that he would be a strong advocate for anti-lynching legislation. To their dismay he was not, fearing a backlash from Southern voters.

In 1934, Senator Edward P. Costigan, a Democrat from Colorado, and Senator Robert F. Wagner, a fellow Democrat from New York, sponsored a bill that would make lynching a federal crime. Among other things it would punish sheriffs who failed to protect prisoners in their custody from attacks by mobs.

In February 1935, hearings on the bill were held in the caucus room of the Senate Office Building before a subcommittee of the Senate Judiciary Committee chaired by Democratic Senator Frederick Van Nuys of California.

Several Marylanders testified. Elisabeth attended as a representative of the Church League for Industrial Democracy, founded in 1905 by social activists, including Professor Vida Scudder whose lectures had inspired her in 1916 to consider becoming a Socialist.

She was in good company. Others who testified with her were: Preston Lane, Jr., then Maryland's Attorney General; Simon E. Soboloff, U.S. District Attorney for Maryland; and three clergymen representing the Maryland Anti-Lynching Federation: Dr. Edward L. Israel, leader of Baltimore's Har Sinai Congregation; the Jesuit Priest, Rev. John T. Gillard, scholar and author ("The Catholic Church and the American Negro", among others); and Rev. Asbury Smith, a Baltimore Methodist who frequently spoke about racial justice issues.

Juanita E. Jackson and Clarence Mitchell represented Baltimore's African-American community. Jackson was National Youth Director of the NAACP. She later became the first African American woman to practice law in Maryland. Mitchell, at the time a reporter for the *Baltimore Afro-American* newspaper, later became the NAACP's chief lobbyist in Washington and one of the architects of federal civil rights legislation. Mitchell had covered the brutal, nighttime lynching, in 1931, of Matthew Williams on the lawn of the Wicomico County courthouse in Salisbury on Maryland's Eastern Shore.

Louis Azrael, a *Baltimore News Post* reporter and columnist, also testified. In a career spanning 60 years, he became known as the Dean of Baltimore journalists.

The bill and other efforts to create anti-lynching laws died in Congress. And, again, President Roosevelt, not wanting to take any chances with the possible loss of Southern votes in the upcoming 1936 election, did nothing to support it.

Elisabeth died 14 years before the landmark Civil Rights Act of 1964 was passed and signed into law by President Lyndon B. Johnson.

Advocating for Spanish Loyalists

Elisabeth was committed to the cause of the Loyalists in the Spanish Civil War in the 1930s, and she served as the financial secretary of the Baltimore branch of the North American Committee to Aid Spanish Democracy. (It may also have been known as American Friends of Spanish Democracy.)

The war (1936-1939) pitted the Republicans (Loyalists)—who were supported by Socialists and Communists and the Soviet Union, Mexico, and foreign volunteers—against the Nationalists, who were supported by the fascist governments of Italy, Germany, and Portugal, as well as foreign volunteer fighters.

Elisabeth and her colleagues from ethnic communities and labor organizations banded together to raise money, food, and supplies for the Loyalists. She recruited many individuals to join the cause, among them Dr. Henry E. Sigerist, director of the Johns Hopkins Institute of the History of Medicine. She asked him to lead a "Physicians Section" of her committee.

Sigerist, in turn, enlisted many of his Hopkins colleagues, including Dr. Adolf Meyer, Hopkins' first psychiatrist-in-chief. Writing to Meyer on December 6, 1936, Sigerist noted:

> It is reported that casualties among the non-combatant population, as a result of the war and epidemics in Madrid and other large centers already run into the tens of thousands, who are getting very little, if any, medical or surgical attention, solely because of the acute storage of supplies.

Elisabeth followed with her own letter to Meyer urging him to get involved with her efforts: "We are very anxious to have you on this committee."

He agreed, as did these other leading Hopkins physicians: Louis Hamman, Samuel Wolman, Ralph Truitt, Earle Moore, Charles Austrian, Horsley Gantt, William Howell, Samuel Morrison, Edwards Park, William Rienhoff, A. Freeman, Simon Solomon, Robert Swain, Hayward Street, and Frank Furstenberg.

At a committee meeting on December 29 at the Hamilton Street Club in downtown Baltimore, the group decided "that an ambulance unit is to be the goal of the local committee. Our publicity shall concern itself with the humanitarian motives in helping the wounded and sick."

They were successful in soliciting local physicians, dentists, pharmacists, and others for $5,000, the amount required to send "a fully equipped ambulance unit from the Baltimore sector to be known as the Baltimore unit. It is to consist of an ambulance, surgical beds, one surgeon, two nurses and two medical orderlies."

In March 1939, in a letter to the *Evening Sun*, Elisabeth described what she called "the facts" about what was happening in Spain and why funds were needed immediately to help those who were opposing the leader of the Nationalists, Francisco Franco.

Citing an "authoritative statement" from her Committee's New York office, Elisabeth said it appeared that a blockade instituted by Franco made it uncertain whether supplies could reach the Loyalists.

More serious, she wrote, was the condition of Republican refugees in France, "one of the most tragic situations in the world today. One loaf of bread per day for twenty-five people; practically no shelter; little protection against disease. Clearly it is our duty to help these millions who fled the Franco terror."

She said the French government desperately needed funds for supplies, food, clothing, and medical supplies. She added that she could only "beg that all friends of these sufferers from Loyalist Spain will send me the most generous possible contributions. They will be forwarded immediately. The goal of the national society is $200,000 by July 19."

The Committee later was described by some as a Communist front linked to the Communist Party USA, but it also has been described as a popular organization that not only attracted Communists but socially minded Christian organizations as well.

All its efforts to support the Republicans failed. The war ended in April 1939. Franco established himself as a repressive dictator.

Johns Hopkins School of Medicine: Jewish Student Quotas?
Sometime during 1935, Elisabeth contacted the Dean of the Johns Hopkins School of Medicine, Dr. Alan Chesney, to tell him that she suspected that the school might be limiting the number of Jewish

students it admitted by using a quota system. She apparently had heard something about such a possibility from a Hopkins student.

Dr. Chesney replied to her in a letter written on December 9, 1935.

> I wonder, [he wrote,] if the professor at the University to whom you referred was properly quoted. I find so often that students are apt to misquote the statements by their instructors.
>
> The Committee on Admissions has never set up any official quota as applied to Jewish students. The percentage of Jewish students admitted varies in fact from year to year. The Committee consists of three men and each makes up his mind independently. The final vote determines if the student is admitted.
>
> If there is one negative vote against an applicant there is apt to be a discussion since one prefers to admit students about whom there would be no question. The choice of students is based not on scholastic record alone but on other qualifications, of which the personal factor is an important one.

Although Elisabeth's response to Dean Chesney, if any, is not to be found, she had every reason to suspect that Hopkins might be limiting the admission of Jewish students to the School of Medicine.

In his book *Bellevue: Three Centuries of Medicine and Mayhem at America's Most Storied Hospital*, historian David Oshinsky has written that medical schools at Cornell, Columbia, Pennsylvania, and Yale had quotas in place. "In 1935 [the same year Elisabeth had written to Chesney] Yale accepted 76 applicants from a pool of 500. About 200 of the applicants were Jewish and only five got in." The Dean's "instructions were remarkably precise," Oshinsky wrote. "'Never admit more than five Jews, take only two Italian Catholics and take no blacks at all.'"

Maryland's Teachers' Oath Bill

In the early to mid-1930s, in legislatures throughout the United States, some right wing politicians advocated strongly for laws that would require teachers in public schools, colleges, and universities (and, in some states, private institutions as well) to sign an oath pledging their loyalty to the constitutions of their state and federal government.

This was in response to the political radicalism of the Depression years and the rising fear that radicals, especially those who were associated with the Communist Party, would infiltrate the nation's education system and subvert it by promoting the ideals and values of Communism. (Organizations like the Pioneer Youth Clubs undoubtedly gave them some cause for concern.)

Patriotic groups like the American Legion and the Daughters of the American Revolution sided with the conservative legislators and endorsed the notion of requiring teachers to sign loyalty oaths.

By 1935, teachers' loyalty oaths were the law in 22 states, with one-third of those states having enacted a loyalty law in that year.

Maryland senators and delegates had jumped on the bandwagon in 1935 and had passed what was called a Teachers' Oath Bill. It had gone to the desk of recently elected Governor Harry Nice for his approval. Elisabeth and many of her liberal friends, especially teachers and professors, were deeply opposed to it.

Her old friend, Joseph S. Ames, now in his final year as president of Johns Hopkins University, accompanied her to a meeting with Governor Nice in Annapolis on April 10, 1935. They urged the governor to veto the legislation. The following day, in a letter addressed to her at 513 Park Avenue, Ames wrote:

My Dear Elisabeth:
    Please let me express to you my sincere appreciation of the

assistance which you have given us in connection with the Teachers' Oath Bill. I thought your speech to the Governor was admirable, and the reference to your father was well timed and I think effective.

In spite of what is said in the paper this morning, I still am hopeful that the Governor will veto the bill.

Governor Nice vetoed the bill when it came to his desk in 1937.

The Non-Sectarian, Non-Political Anti-Nazi Emergency Committee

In 1936, Elisabeth rallied others to join her in protesting Nazi activities in Germany. Writing to a friend, she said, "We received such a favorable response for the Protest Meeting that it has been decided to hold it this Wednesday, April 29, 8:00 p.m. at Lehman Hall. Gerhart Seger, former Reichstag member and liberal editor, will be the chief speaker. Urge your friends to attend."

Christian Colleges in China

In late 1937, Elisabeth sent an invitation to a group of friends to come to her home on December 7 for a meeting "in behalf of the Christian Colleges of China." She said the speakers would be Dr. Edward Hume, an alumnus of the Hopkins School of Medicine and one of the early leaders of the Yale-in-China program "now of the Christian Medical Council for Overseas work." The other speaker was "Dr. Chi ch'ao-ting of the Institute of Pacific Relations."

She added "There will be no solicitation of funds," a nod to the fact she usually was asking friends for financial support for one organization or another.

The Workers' Defense League

In December 1942, Elisabeth was working hard to raise money

for the Workers' Defense League (WDL). Instead of sending her friends her traditional Christmas greeting, she asked them to send money to the WDL.

The big job The Workers' Defense League has been doing throughout the country: working with Negro, labor and church groups against race discrimination in jobs and voting. We need to raise $1,000 in cash and pledges by December so the staff can know that their friends are sticking with them and will see to it that they can keep up their vital work. If you agree that this job of fighting Fascism at home is worth doing and want to help the Workers Defense League unite labor, Negro, church and liberal groups in doing that job, make your check out to this organization and route it through me, and so help give me a Merry Christmas.

CHAPTER 29

THE RUN FOR SENATE/1934

In the spring of 1934, Maryland was gearing up once again for statewide elections. And the Socialists chose their candidates, as they had before, at a convention in Hagerstown. This time Elisabeth was nominated to run for the United State Senate. Her friend, the social activist professor at Johns Hopkins, Dr. Broadus Mitchell, would be the Party's candidate for Governor.

Following a course similar to the one she chose when running for governor four years earlier, Elizabeth left the country in mid-July for a six-week trip to Europe. She wanted to recharge her batteries and to check on Socialist activities in England and on the continent.

On her return, in early September, she told an *Evening Sun* reporter that she had a "feeling of the tremendous reaction against Fascism in both France and England." She was appalled by a riot at a meeting where a pro-fascist member of Parliament, Sir Oswald Mosley, was speaking. Protesters were objecting to his speech and he called out his "Black Shirts" to disperse them. She said, "women and children were beaten brutally."

(Mosley, a conservative member of Parliament who was wealthy, handsome, and a charismatic speaker, had become convinced that Great Britain should adopt a Fascist form of government similar to that practiced in Italy at the time. Whenever he spoke publicly on this subject he was besieged by mobs who opposed him. For protection and to allow the meetings to be held, he employed a gang of thugs, dressed in black shirts, to disperse the opposition. They did so, sometimes violently.)

Elisabeth concluded her interview with the *Evening Sun* by saying she was "full of energy for the coming campaign." She was 67 years old.

During the campaign she had a ready-made opportunity to grab some local headlines.

The City of Baltimore was planning to hold a pageant to celebrate the State's Tercentenary. The organizers had invited many countries to send representatives to participate in the opening ceremonies and carry their national flags. Germany was to be represented and marchers planned to carry two flags—the German national flag and the flag of the Nazi Party.

Elisabeth was incensed. Allowing this to happen, she said, in a *Baltimore Sun* article, "is giving tacit approval to the spirit of intolerance and persecution for which the [Nazi] emblem stands at the time when Maryland is celebrating the spirit of tolerance on which the State was founded."

The organizers permitted the German contingent to carry the Nazi flag, giving Elisabeth another opportunity to state her opposition in the local media. "The Nazi emblem has meant the destruction of democracy, the violation of religious liberty, the denial of free speech and other civil rights, the crushing of the free labor movement and the terrorist persecution of all opposition," she noted.

Her campaign took her to all parts of the state—out west to

Oakland and up to Port Deposit, with many stops in various Balti-more neighborhoods and at luncheons and dinners, where she often shared the platform with gubernatorial candidate Broadus Mitchell.

On July 4, speaking at Workmen's Circle Park, Elisabeth gave an impassioned patriotic, anti-Fascist, anti-war talk that was also pro-civil rights and pro-Socialist. The newspaper headline over the article reporting her remarks summed it up: "The Workers Must Fight Fascism and War."

She argued strongly on behalf of the state's black citizens, saying that discrimination had to be stopped. She cited the color barrier at the Maryland Institute (now the Maryland Institute College of Art) saying that "colored people of Maryland" should be allowed to attend the well-respected art college in Baltimore.

She pressed for the building of a high school for black students in Baltimore County, noting that only 65 black students from the county attended Baltimore's Douglass High School because parents of other black students in the county could not afford the cost of transporting them to the city.

She said it was discriminatory and unfair for the whites-only Towson State Normal School to offer a four-year program of study while students at the historically black Bowie State Normal School only received three years of education.

In the end, of course, the Socialists earned only a fraction of the total vote in the 1935 election. Broadus Mitchell received 4,674 votes and Elisabeth received 4,094 votes, according to the *Sun*.

In a small but humorous, post-election column headlined "Post-Mortem," *Sun* writers presented a list of predictions, such as:

> No creditable cure will be found for baldness.
> Tobacco will burn pipe smokers' tongues.
> The Orioles will look like a winning aggregation early in the season.

The oboist will sound a sour note occasionally.

And, finally: "Dr. Broadus Mitchell and Miss Lizzie Gilman will find something else to run for."

Throughout 1934, Elisabeth found time to paste admiring clippings from "letters to the editor" into her now faded avocado-colored scrapbook.

"H.G." commended the *Sun* for an editorial about her. "A fine tribute to a fine person."

Henry A. Rogers told the *Sun*'s editors that they "deserve a pat on the back for your fine editorial … concerning Miss Elisabeth Gilman … I find myself almost in complete accord with her as far as economics is concerned."

Elias Wingate took the *Sun* to task for publishing a letter in which a writer had criticized her. The person had said, "I think they ought to shut Miss Gilman's mouth." Saying no one has done more "to make this town a better place to live," Mr. Wingate concluded: "She is a great person."

Prominent in her scrapbook is a handwritten letter, in pencil, signed by "A Old Friend" [sic].

If you could only realize you are a disgrace to your late and esteemed father whom Balto and the world admired. If you had half his brains, you would direct them for good issues and be a good American and not a vile troublemaker. Go to Russia, stay there. Siberia is the place for you. It's vile notoriety you want, you old troublemaker… You are beyond decency. So hurry over and live with the Russians. You know the customs there.

She must have chuckled as she pasted it in her scrapbook.

CHAPTER 30

RUNNING FOR MAYOR, SENATOR, SHERIFF, AND GOVERNOR (AGAIN)

E arly in 1935, Elisabeth was running for public office again—
this time for mayor of Baltimore.

One might have thought that by now she would have grown
tired of campaigning, of telling the public about the virtues of
Socialism, of "doing the right thing" for working men and women—
exposing capitalists and public officials whom she believed were
feathering their own nests at the expense of the people.

But she seems to have been more energized than ever.

She was nominated for mayor at a Socialist Party meeting in
Baltimore on the evening of January 31, 1935. The next day the
Sun announced "Socialists Give Miss Gilman Nomination For
Mayoralty." The article was accompanied by a stock photo of Elisabeth that the paper had used many times. She was looking slightly
to the left, wearing a dark jacket with lapel pin, a white blouse, a
round dark hat pulled down over her forehead and wearing large,
round glasses, giving her eyes a somewhat owlish look.

The paper described "the things she would do if she were Mayor."

… Establish municipally owned dairies, bakers, coal yards, markets, ice plants, where products can be supplied at reasonable prices.

… Eliminate all frame, portable schools.

… Erect and maintain at low rentals modern homes and apartments for working people to replace the slums in which a large number of our citizens live.

… Establish municipal ownership and distribution of gas, steam heat and electric power to be supplied at or near the cost of production.

… Establish a modern system of motorbus transportation, municipally owned and operated, with a 5-cent fare.

True to her nature, Elisabeth opened her campaign on April 6 by joining a picket line composed of striking clothing workers. As they walked along Pratt Street, a squad of local policemen insisted that they keep moving.

Someone shouted from the sidewalk: What's your platform?" She replied at once "Solidarity for labor," accentuating her point with a "gaily colored feather on her hat that jiggled with the motion of her head," a *Sun* reporter wrote.

The marchers cheered, jeered and sang as Miss Gilman announced her platform. And amid the din [she] raised her hand and with a wavering motion, added: "Industrial as well as political democracy."

And local citizens, writing to the *Sun*, continued to praise her. S.B. Charles thanked the editors for "giving her and her party prominence in your great paper." He continued:

We hardly can appreciate her worth. She is at the forefront in every worth-while movement in our community… A vote for Miss Gilman and the other Socialist candidates will mean a step in the direction of a finer civilization.

Elisabeth had long been an advocate of municipally owned transportation systems, which charged riders the lowest possible fares. At the time she was running for mayor she was presented with a serious transportation issue in Baltimore.

United Railways, the privately owned operator of the city's trolley system, was going bankrupt and was about to be sold at public auction. In earlier days Elisabeth might have argued that the city take over the business. But not this time.

Writing a column in the *Sun* on February 20, 1935, "A Socialist Looks at The Rapid Transit Situation," she noted,

> I am strongly in favor of municipal ownership—but in the case of United Railways, where the financial condition is so precarious, I am distinctly opposed to having such an important program as municipal ownership jeopardized, and perhaps in the end, fail, through no fault of the fundamental plan. I say let United "be hoisted on its own petard!

She cited many problems and inconveniences caused by trolley service in the city and said the transit system was a patchwork and obsolescent system that ought to be abandoned. "Plan for an entirely new city-owned bus system!" she advised.

She proposed a detailed plan to bring buses into the community. Her conclusion was that such systems had worked well in other cities and that "it can be done here, it will be done here, if the citizens of Baltimore unite for their own good in voting for the Socialist Mayor and City Councilmen."

Despite her efforts and the activity of her Socialist Party activists,

Elisabeth lost this election as she had lost others. Some 2,440 Baltimoreans cast their votes for her.

Undaunted, Elisabeth had other fish to fry.

In June 1936, she took a brief trip north to Philadelphia to support striking Arkansas cotton sharecroppers who were demonstrating at the 1936 Democratic National Convention in that city.

Elisabeth, representing the League for Industrial Democracy, joined 100 others on a picket line to bring to the convention delegates their concerns about the poor treatment of the sharecroppers and to seek their support for the striking members of the Southern Tenant Farmers Union.

Earlier she had written President Roosevelt asking that he order the Justice Department to investigate what she called "the terrorization" of the sharecroppers. The White House assured her that the Justice Department would investigate the situation.

1938: Campaign for Senator

In August 1938, the Socialists once again wanted to be present in the campaign that would elect a United States senator from Maryland. They asked Elisabeth to permit them to nominate her as their candidate.

Even though she was approaching her 71st birthday, Elisabeth agreed to let her name go forward as a candidate for the U.S. Senate. It was her second attempt and the fifth time she had run for public office in Maryland. She engaged in a brief campaign, which opened in mid-September and, as in the past, received far too few votes to win.

1942: Campaigning for Sheriff

In the elections of 1942, the Socialists wanted to fill a slate of candidates for municipal offices and tapped Elisabeth to be their candidate for sheriff of Baltimore.

An article in the *Sun*'s Sunday edition of August 2, 1942, announced that Elisabeth had filed for the office. It was accompanied by photos of the current sheriff, Joseph C. Deegan, and Elisabeth. Deegan, described as 6-feet, 2-inches tall, is seen standing to his full height, wearing a long overcoat and fedora hat, while the diminutive Elisabeth is shown in a striped blouse leaning over a large basket containing her three pet dogs—all chows.

The editors decided to have fun with the story and headlined the article, "Woman May Have to Perform Job of Whipping Wife Beater" and a sub-headline: "That Is If Miss Elisabeth Gilman is Elected to Sheriff's Office on the Socialist Party Ticket."

One of the duties of sheriffs in Maryland, at that time, was "to administer, under their own hand, lashes 'not to exceed forty' which are the legal penalty for wife-beating in the state," according to the *Sun*. "And so, should she be elected," the *Sun* wrote, "and should a wife-beater be convicted and sentenced to twenty lashes and six months, Miss Gilman, who has fought all her life for liberalism and enlightenment, would have to deliver the lashes.

"Miss Gilman, a small woman of 75, friends believe, wouldn't like that at all."

The *Sun* tried to contact Elisabeth for comment, but she was not in town. Friends said she was in New England for the summer. Before any campaign she always found time to go away for a rest in anticipation of the arduous days ahead.

When she returned to Baltimore in October her first public statements drew immediate attention.

She said that if elected she would urge that the office of sheriff be abolished in favor of a non-elected administrator. But in the meantime, she said that the Sheriff's office should be more aggressive in its protection of the rights of accused persons. If elected, she said, she would "devote special attention to the rights of women and negroes."

Her opponent was reelected by a wide margin.

1945: Campaigning for Governor (Again)

Over the years, Elisabeth and a Socialist colleague, William A. Toole, often had run for office together, one seeking the Governor's office, the other the Senate. Their commitment was to keep the Socialist Party on the ballot and to have a public platform to trumpet the virtues and principles of the Party.

In 1945, Elisabeth, then almost 78, was the Socialists' choice for Governor—again. Toole was the candidate for Senate.

Interviewed by the *Sun*, she was characteristically straightforward. "I frankly admit that I don't think I have a chance in the world of being elected. I am running for office to spread the Socialist point of view.

"Mine will be an educational campaign, educational, that is, for the voters of Maryland who will be given a chance to hear about and think about the various issues I'll raise."

And she asked Marylanders to think carefully about her platform:

... A workable peace within the present framework of United Nations cooperation, a peace with a primary economic basis.

... Emphasis on Civil Liberties.

... Full employment.

... Equal rights for Negroes."

In the end, William Preston Lane, a Democrat, was elected Governor.

Just prior to her campaign, the *Sun* printed a long and laudatory—one might call it affectionate—editorial on October 15, 1945.

It was headlined "Part of the Tradition."

> Miss Gilman represents the Socialist Party, to be sure, [the editors
> wrote,] but under her personal leadership it has become both more
> and less than a political party seeking, always seeking, office, it is
> part of a Maryland tradition, indigenous, respected and partaking
> of the comfortable force of local custom.
>
> Miss Gilman, the news stories recall, is now 78. Who in our State
> can remember a time when she was not upholding her chosen cause
> with dignity and a reasonableness which are as natural to her as the
> long ardor and faithfulness with which she has canvassed in behalf
> of her political beliefs, with a hopefulness in which there is no atom
> of self-seeking or self-deception.

The editors concluded:

> Miss Gilman will not be returned to the governorship, nor more than
> she has been returned in the past to the governorship, the mayoralty,
> the Senate or the Sheriff's post. None knows it better than she.
>
> But there are few Marylanders and still fewer Baltimoreans who,
> without the least attention to her party, will fail to welcome her, as
> emerging unwearied and undiscouraged from her Park Avenue
> home, she enters the campaign once more.

It would be her last campaign.

CHAPTER 31

THE RELATIONSHIP COOLS

Though Elisabeth and Mercer continued to correspond and meet for business throughout the 1930s and into the 1940s, their relationship gradually cooled and they eventually drifted apart.

Interestingly and curiously, there is no indication that she and Mercer corresponded about her political ventures. She apparently did not inform him about her intentions to run for various public offices and, if he knew what she was doing, he did not write to her about it.

Most correspondence typically went from Elisabeth to Mercer. Her notes related to Christian Social Justice Fund business or issues related to the Open Forum. And, from time to time, there were sentimental notes about the time they had spent together in France during World War I.

Whenever Mercer initiated contact he usually wanted something from her, or to express concern about his job or his or Katherine's health.

Early in 1932, Mercer's Peoples' Legislative Service failed. He wrote:

Dear Elisabeth: The enclosures will tell you why you did not receive a request from the PLS for the renewal of their contribution from the CSJF... For the past two months absolutely all the energy I could summon has been devoted to trying to avert what has now come to pass in the affairs of the PLS, that first, and then the big, task of getting the organization decently and quietly interred.

There have been various time consuming complications to be straightened out...in settling the affairs of an eleven-year-old organization whose chief servant has assumed the somewhat ambitious job of trying not only to save his own country but the world!

In mid-January 1934, Mercer told Elisabeth that he had taken a job created under the National Recovery Act, working with electric power utilities. He was unhappy and constantly in fear of losing his job because of his opposition to "the power trust."

I have been working with all my might for several weeks, 12 to 15 hours a day to frustrate the sinister purposes of people in the power industry and administration. There is nothing whatsoever in this Electric Light and Power Code, either for Labor or the Public. From start to finish it is a Power Trust Code.

I am doing work of real value. I am meeting face to face, and battling and coming to know firsthand the representatives of the forces of greed. I am constantly being struck at. Week before last I was almost struck down. I am marked for sacrifice. Sometimes my every word is watched and weighed.

Elisabeth responded calmly and with spiritual encouragement on January 25: "I am very sorry to hear from you, what I knew last week...that your work and position are in danger. You did escape from Death Valley and there is also hope that you may be allowed to function where you are."

Mercer remained as an employee of the federal government until he retired some years later.

Typical of Elisabeth's nostalgia for their days in France was a letter she wrote to Mercer in February 1935: She sent him a copy of a letter, in French, from one Victor Mongin. "We will never forget, will we, the little boy behind the bread counter, and to think that he has been manager now for four years of one of the best hotels in Chamonix."

In 1936, the trustees of the Christian Social Justice Fund (CSJF) snubbed Mercer once again.

He had sent Elisabeth, as secretary/treasurer of the Fund, an appeal from the Public Ownership League, which was advocating the public ownership of utilities. Mercer recommended the CSJF award $1,000 to the league. Four of the five trustees, including Elisabeth, voted against his request.

There is no indication in the papers of Elisabeth or Mercer that they corresponded at all in 1938. They probably saw each other, perhaps infrequently, at board meetings of the CSJF held in Baltimore.

In November 1939, Elisabeth wrote, "It is very long since I have had word from you and Katherine. I trust you are both well and could come over some weekend." She invited Mercer to participate in one of the Open Forum meetings to help celebrate the organization's 25th anniversary year. There is no indication that he attended or that they visited her at 513 Park Avenue.

Early in January 1940, at the bottom of a formal notice of a CSJF board meeting, she added, in a handwritten note, "Personal greetings to K. If you can, stay for the night at 513. There are early trains to Washington."

In December, while thanking the Johnstons for their Christmas card, she said she was sorry to learn that Mercer had had some sort of accident. "I am distressed about it but trust you are going to be able to make a complete recovery."

As she had done so many times in the past, she offered financial support.

I hope I am right in my supposition that you are not financially embarrassed. If you were I should hope to be able to send you some more tangible proof of my friendship.

I myself am housed with a broken ankle…but my sister has rented a wheelchair for me which will be nice for the holidays. With affectionate greetings to you both, Yours as ever, Elisabeth Gilman.

About a year later, Elisabeth wrote:

My dear Katherine and Mercer:

In going over my papers, I found quite a number from you both. One of our friends says that after 70 years we are living on borrowed time. Although I am feeling extremely well, I am trying to wind up a certain accumulation of various materials. One of our aunts used to say that burning was an honorable death for records etc. but do as you think wise about what I am sending you.

Presumably these items are correspondence between them that Katherine Johnston placed with the Mercer Green Johnston Papers in the Library of Congress. Elisabeth's files in the Hamburger Archives contain none of their correspondence.

CHAPTER 32

MOVING FROM 513 PARK AVENUE

In the spring of 1941, Elisabeth decided to leave her home of 30 years at 513 Park Avenue and to move a block north to 614 Park Avenue, a house that earlier had belonged to her parents.

It must have been a difficult decision to leave her large gracious home of twelve rooms and four baths—a classic Victorian home, with floor-to-ceiling windows on the first floor and a heavy, dark wood-trimmed interior.

The residence at 513 Park not only had piled memory upon memory for Elisabeth, but Baltimoreans knew it well and remembered the many events held there that had made such an impact on the city's social and political life.

For her part, Elisabeth said, the most exciting gathering there was the dinner for Oswald Garrison Villard, whom she had invited to the city to celebrate the tenth anniversary of his becoming editor of *The Nation*. The event, for more than 100 people, had been held at 513 Park because some of Baltimore's black citizens had been invited to the celebration and no banquet hall in the city would accommodate a mixed race gathering. So, at the last minute, Elisabeth had invited everyone to her home.

Some of her happiest gatherings, she said, were the luncheons she held for guests who spoke at the Sunday afternoon Open Forum meetings.

Her guest book overflowed with autographs of prominent individuals:

- Arthur Garfield Hays and Roger Baldwin, leaders of the Civil Rights Union;
- Judge John M. Woolsey, who handed down the decision by which James Joyce's "Ulysses" was admitted for sale in the United States in 1933.
- The Johns Hopkins professor, Broadus Mitchell, a friend and Socialist running mate, was a frequent guest.
- Nationally recognized Socialists like Norman Thomas, Eugene Debs, and Dr. Harry W. Laidler often visited.
- The poet, Edwin Markham had come to 513 Park, as had the Irish poet Patrick Quinlan, and the painter, Kendall Saunders.
- The Maryland Committee on Civil Liberties was founded at 513 Park Avenue.
- So was the short-lived coterie of liberals, the Fabian Club, which also held its meetings there.

Two things probably stimulated Elisabeth to move. One was the declining character of the immediate neighborhood. Once one of the most exclusive addresses in the city, it was just around the corner from the Washington Monument, the Peabody Conservatory of Music, and the Walters Art Museum. But by 1941, many of the adjacent Victorian mansions had been torn down to make way for commercial buildings and parking lots. A parking lot had been built beside 513. The second, and more important reason for Elisabeth to move, was that her sister, Alice, had purchased

614 Park Avenue where their parents had lived. Nowhere among Elisabeth's papers is there any reference to the details of the transaction or why Alice decided to make the purchase.

Perhaps she only wanted to help Elisabeth escape the deteriorating conditions around 513 Park, or perhaps she and Elisabeth had a sentimental attachment to the house at 614.

Alice's husband, Everett Wheeler, had died. He was a wealthy New York attorney and one might imagine that he had provided well for her.

Alice never lived at 614 Park. She remained at her home in New York City and visited Elisabeth occasionally. She retained ownership of the property until she died in 1945. She bequeathed it to Elisabeth and, in addition, gave her a life interest in a $50,000 trust. The principal of the trust was designated for Johns Hopkins after Elisabeth's death.

The sale of 513 Park was covered widely in the Baltimore press.

One of the *Sun*'s columnists, Jon O'Ren, writing in a series called "Down the Spillway," expressed the sentiments of many of his fellow journalists and his readers upon learning of the sale. Some excerpts from his May 10, 1941, column:

He described 513 "not simply as a residence, it is a headquarters building, the center for many years of local movements that are, if I may risk a bilingual pun, left, but not sinister.

Baltimore has been skeptical of Miss Lizzie's ideas, but I do not believe that any rational Baltimorean doubts her patriotism; politically she has carried a sting but never a pollard, and not a few of the conferences and consultations that have taken place at 513 Park Avenue have contributed to the good life of the city, if only in creating a healthier tolerance of differences we might not have had without these meetings...

The Park Avenue house, to me, seemed to express with extraordinary perfection, much of what was best in the life of the Victorian period…It is the house of a generation that, at its best, was certain of itself and of its place in the world, tranquil, cultivated, upright in its dealings…

Her removal means, I fear, the disappearance of one more remnant, not merely of old Baltimore, but of the particularly fine old Baltimore whose loss all men lament.

Despite these sentiments 513 was later demolished. The Gilman home at 614 Park Avenue was, too—torn down less than a year after Elisabeth died in December 1950. Title had passed to Johns Hopkins University following her death. Despite a few local protests that it was a property worth preserving, university officials, according to an *Evening Sun* account on November 14, 1951, said that the financial return on the property would be "considerably more" as a parking lot than if it were sold or used for university purposes.

CHAPTER 33

PRESERVING HER FATHER'S LEGACY

Throughout her life, Elisabeth would find specific ways to preserve her father's legacy to be certain that he was given the honor and respect she believed he deserved.

In 1910, two years after her father's death, Elisabeth criticized the Hopkins trustees for not acting promptly enough to create a suitable memorial to him. When the trustees of Baltimore's Country School for Boys sought her permission to name the school for her father, she readily agreed. Her motivation may have been prompted by her unhappiness with the Hopkins trustees but she also would have recalled that her father had encouraged the formation of the school in the late 1890s.

Only after she agreed to let the school be named for her father did she inform the president of the Hopkins board of trustees, R. Brent Keyser, that she had accepted The Country School's proposal.

Keyser responded in a two-and-a-half page letter, written on university stationery and dated December 15, 1910. Keyser wrote that "immediately after your father's death an effort was made to raise funds for a suitable memorial to him at Homewood. In view of the fact that Homewood was at that time, and practically still is, entirely undeveloped…this movement was not then successful."

Keyser said that the sooner the original Howard Street campus in downtown Baltimore could be closed and removed to Homewood the sooner trustees would be able "to secure a proper memorial." Then Keyser told Elisabeth that he had visited with her mother shortly after Gilman's death and that he had an agreement with her that the Gilman name would not be used elsewhere without approval of the university trustees.

Referring to the early attempt to raise money for a Gilman memorial, he wrote,

> At the time the first effort was made to raise the fund, your mother sent for me and, after learning the situation, said she would not consent to any other use of the name until the university had first had an opportunity to carry out its own plans, unless we would give our consent to her doing so.

Keyser expressed the "great disappointment" the trustees felt because they were "unable to realize their intention of honoring the university by a suitable memorial to Mr. Gilman."

He concluded that while the trustees

> do not agree as to the propriety of the present use of your father's name in connection with the Country School, we of course respect the wishes of yourself and your sister…The committee is therefore writing Dr. Joseph S. Ames, President of The Country School, that we withdraw all objection to the use of Mr. Gilman's name…

(Ames was a distinguished professor of physics at Hopkins who later would become president of the university.)

Keyser and the Hopkins trustees may have been among the first in Baltimore to recognize that Elisabeth was someone unafraid to stand up for what she believed to be a correct course of action, whether or not someone else agreed.

The Flexner Biography of Gilman

In 1926, Elisabeth was working again to burnish her father's legacy. She was seeking someone to write a new biography of her father. An earlier one had been written by Fabian Franklin, a mathematics professor at Hopkins, but perhaps she wanted something more laudatory or written in a style more to her liking, or written by one whose record in the academy was more distinguished than Franklin's.

Among others she sought the advice of one of her father's old Hopkins colleagues, John J. Abel, the world-famous pharmacologist.

In a letter to him she wrote: "As you know the biography of my father by Dr. Franklin hardly covers the matter, as few people had the opportunity that my father had of helping to organize the Sheffield Scientific School, the University of California, the Johns Hopkins University and the Carnegie Institution."

Whatever her reason may have been, she approached Dr. Abraham Flexner, whom she knew, and asked him to do a new biography of her father.

Flexner, while on the research staff of the Carnegie Foundation for the Advancement of Teaching, had researched, written and, in 1910, published a report entitled "Medical Education in the United States and Canada." It triggered much needed reforms in the standards, organization, and curricula of medical schools. Based on the report, Flexner became a household name among university leaders, especially those who were interested in medical education.

Elisabeth had chosen someone whose reputation for exceptional research and scholarship were second to none. And she knew that Flexner held her father in the highest esteem. She wanted him to write the biography and she would not give up until he had done it.

Seemingly on the basis of a conversation they had, Flexner wrote Elisabeth on April 8, 1935. He wanted to impress upon her that he was exceedingly busy with the new Institute for Advanced Study at Princeton, N.J., of which he was the founding director in 1930. He wrote:

> I quite understand your feeling of filial piety urges you not to delay in the matter of providing a proper biography of your father. Unfortunately, the organization of the Institute has been such an absorbing task that I have not been able to give my mind to anything else.

Flexner probably made a mistake. He led Elisabeth to believe that he would write the biography.

He wrote: "There is nothing I would rather do than prepare a memorial volume of the kind you and I have discussed." That was exactly what Elisabeth wanted to hear and it was all that she needed to keep pressure on him to produce the biography, no matter how long it might take.

Eight months after receiving that small bit of encouragement from him, on January 2, 1936, Elisabeth wrote to tell him that she had "certain manuscripts" which she wanted to send him and "anything I have is at your disposal…"

Two weeks later, on January 16, Flexner acknowledged her letter and wrote that his

> desire to write your father's biography is as strong as ever, but I am so enmeshed in the affairs of the new Institute that I still cannot

find the leisure to turn to it.

I think I may be having the same experience which your father had in the early days of Johns Hopkins. The Institute, like Hopkins, is relatively a small affair, but the time and energy it consumes are out of all proportion to its size. I shall communicate with you whenever the pressure upon me relaxes.

Elisabeth acknowledged his letter with, "Of course I am disappointed that you have not found leisure yet." She went on to mention that she had found a reference in one of her father's notebooks to a Mr. Goodyear.

That to me means the Goodyear Rubber Company, for I had heard my father had received a very generous offer to work for them. What a different life he would have had as a business executive!—and I cannot but think how different higher education would have been in the U.S.A.

She concluded the letter with

I think you realize that we do not want a large volume on the subject which would take a great deal of your time and might not be read by younger people who did not know my father—but a comparatively short study of his work in education ...and you will find the leisure time to take it up.

On January 22, Flexner wrote that he "feels badly" that he has not kept his promise to write the biography but that he still wanted to do it, adding "On the other hand I have passed my seventieth year ..." and "I am conscious of the fact that anything may happen to a person who has reached this stage."

He told her that if she were willing to wait a bit longer, "I shall be more than happy to make good my promise." But, perhaps looking for a way to wiggle out of the assignment, he wrote "If, however, you feel that the task is one that should not be postponed, I hope that you will feel perfectly free to try to find someone else who is thoroughly competent to do it."

Although Elisabeth did not take the bait, it seems clear that he was asking to be excused from this assignment.

Until that time he had not told her that he was writing another biography!

In a letter to her on February 15, 1936, he said that was writing a biography of Dr. (William H.) Welch, "a formidable task taken at the request of the trustees of the Johns Hopkins University and Dr. Welch's intimate relatives."

Welch was one of the founding "big four" doctors of Johns Hopkins Medicine.

If Elisabeth were shocked or disappointed by this news there is no correspondence indicating that. Indeed, when Flexner asked her to send him any recollections of Dr. Welch, or copies of letters between them, she replied immediately.

February 17, 1936:

I shall never forget the great help he was at a small protest meeting held at my house in behalf of Sacco and Vanzetti. The phraseology of the protest was difficult but Dr. Welch and two others worked it out admirably. I remember he quoted to me Voltaire's statement that however greatly he differed from an opponent he maintained his fundamental right to be heard.

She added, "I recollect with pleasure how he used to give me $100 a year for my 'boys' club,' as he so greatly approved of baseball, a sport in which they delighted."

Correspondence went back and forth between Elisabeth and Flexner for another two years.

On July 6, 1938, he wrote,

I feel guilty, though I also feel that I have a good defense. During the last two or three years fully half my time has been devoted to efforts in behalf of displaced scholars from Germany and now from Austria, but for these I should have carried out my promise to you long ago.

He adds,

I have the feeling that Dr. (Fabian) Franklin has done the biographical part admirably but that now we can see in perspective your father's importance, and I may say, that in my opinion, his importance grows with the passing years.

Such words must have strengthened Elisabeth's hope that no matter how long it took, the manuscript Flexner would produce would be worth the wait.

Flexner completed his 173-page Gilman biography in 1946, more than ten years after Elisabeth's first conversations with him about it. It was published by Harcourt, Brace and Company, under the title, *Daniel Coit Gilman, Creator of the American Type of University*.

In his preface Flexner wrote "I have long desired to write a book about Daniel Coit Gilman, but until quite recently, I could not find the leisure.

The reader will find in this volume an outline of Gilman's life only in so far as it explains his influence on American education. It has been made possible by a grant from The Carnegie Corporation of New York to the Carnegie Foundation for the Advancement of Teaching."

He acknowledged the assistance of many at Johns Hopkins and Elisabeth.

But her name was misspelled; a "z" was used instead of "s," an error Elisabeth had seen many times throughout her life.

CHAPTER 34

TESTIMONIAL DINNER

In November 1941, when Elisabeth was nearly 74 years old, friends from Baltimore and around the country decided it was time to pay public tribute for her life of service to dozens of liberal causes and to the political life of Maryland and the nation.

It is not clear why they chose to honor her at that particular time. Perhaps her decision to move away from her longtime home at 513 Park Avenue earlier in the year led some to believe that she was about to withdraw from her day-to-day commitment to the social causes that she had championed for so many years.

If the sponsors of the dinner thought that Elisabeth was about to retire from public life, they were wrong. She still had political races to run—for Sheriff of Baltimore in 1942 and, once again, for Governor of Maryland in 1945. And her work with organizations like The Fellowship of Reconciliation, the League for Industrial Democracy, and the Women's International League for Peace and Freedom continued just as before.

But testimonial dinners often serve the interests of those in attendance almost as much as they honor an individual. Memories filled with nostalgia and recollections of accomplishments, and disappointments, can help to assemble a crowd and make their salute to the honoree even more compelling and satisfying. And that may have been the case at the dinner honoring Elisabeth.

More than 500 persons, paying $1.75 each, gathered at Baltimore's popular Southern Hotel on the evening of November 5 to cheer on their old friend. The Southern, of course, was the same hotel that had denied the use of its dining facilities, on racial grounds, for the Villard dinner some years earlier.

Norman Thomas, the perennial Socialist candidate for President, was there. So was the Rector of Old St. Paul's Church, Elisabeth's pastor for 30 years, Rev. Arthur B. Kinsolving, and Johns Hopkins professor Broadus Mitchell, her longtime Socialist running mate and close friend.

Rabbi Adolph Coblenz, the distinguished leader of Chizuk Amunu, one of Baltimore's oldest Jewish congregations was present, as was Harry Greenstein, executive director of the Associated Jewish Charities.

Dr. Adolf Meyer, the pioneering psychiatrist and former director of the Phipps Clinic at Johns Hopkins Hospital, her close friend, was there. So were two prominent attorneys: Judge Joseph N. Ulman, a leading spokesman for prison reform; and former U.S. Attorney, Simon Sobeloff, later to become U.S. Solicitor General and Chief Judge of the U. S. Court of Appeals for the Fourth Circuit.

Dr. George Murphy, secretary of the board of the *Afro-American* newspaper and a member of the Baltimore Housing Authority, was a prominent guest, as was Edward S. Lewis, executive director of the Baltimore Urban League. He praised Elisabeth for not approaching black citizens "in a spirit of paternalism."

Sadly, for Elisabeth, her friends of twenty-five years, Mercer and Katherine Johnston, were not in attendance. A few days before the event, Mercer wrote to her:

Dear Elisabeth: I regret that my plans to be with you at the dinner in your honor ... have been upset by plans of the Rural Electrical Administration which failed to take my plans into account.

I hope the occasion will be all that your heart could desire. ... You have done good—especially the out-of-the-way kind—for upwards of a quarter-century, freely, zealously, generously and you are still going strong.

Katherine joins me in drinking, in spirit, to the toasts of the evening. Yours sincerely, Mercer.

Noticeably absent, also, were her political opponents from earlier years. Only one, Mayor Howard W. Jackson, responded to the invitation and even he said he had a previous engagement that evening but would "try to stop by." If he did, none of the newspaper writers covering the dinner mentioned his presence.

Johns Hopkins economics professor Sidney Hollander opened the speaking part of the program by saying he was taking the place of the Rev. Dr. Edward L. Israel, formerly Rabbi of Har Sinai Congregation, who had died suddenly a few days earlier. Hollander read a message from the Rabbi's widow who said Elisabeth and her husband had "worked and wrought together in common purpose."

Professor Hollander said that the dinner was composed of "representatives of the Blue Book and the Red Network, Socialists and socialites." He called Elisabeth "one of America's grandest institutions. She stirred Baltimore as Einstein stirred the universe."

Loud applause followed Hollander's remark that "Baltimore was entitled to one Liberal. For years we followed her causes, some of them cock-eyed, which were, by later development, not so cock-eyed."

Norman Thomas said the various interests represented among the audience were so diversified that there "is so much potential dynamite in the room that anything can happen here."

He commended Elisabeth for "the fact that she did not say different things at different times to different people. Hers has been a naturalism of action and an unassuming integrity. She assumed that if a thing were wrong it could be set right."

Thomas found it amusing that, "Here she sits with orchids on and she is a Socialist."

Concluding the program, Elisabeth told how she had worked with social service organizations for many years before becoming a Socialist. "I worked with organizations that were not radical in the best sort of way, but they were not getting at the roots of things. We Socialists want a better place for everyone to live in."

She closed her brief remarks by warning her audience, "As war threatens, keep guard on civil liberties."

A month later, the Japanese bombed Pearl Harbor.

The *Evening Sun*'s editors added their own tribute the day after the banquet, in an article headlined, "Miss Gilman's Dinner."

There are testimonial dinners and testimonial dinners, but too few like last night's occasion in honor of Miss Elisabeth Gilman, indefatigable liberal, reformer and Hound of Heaven extraordinary. Miss Gilman proved the catalytic agent which drew charming and graceful addresses from all sorts of people. Some of the guests probably were bursting to pass on from Miss Gilman to stirring discussion of the evils of the day. Perhaps others, if pressed, would have admitted that only a small minority of Miss Gilman's many causes made a strong appeal to them. But, given Miss Gilman herself and the energy, cheerfulness and good temper with which she has pursued her objectives and persuaded or dynamited others to join her, all could join in making Miss Gilman's dinner the brilliant and touching success which it was.

CHAPTER 35

ELISABETH'S DEATH

Elisabeth had fallen and broken her hip during the summer of 1947. She recuperated over a period of five months, inactive for most of that time. Finally, with grit and determination, she was able to walk once again.

Her nurse and companion from the time of her fall until she died was Anne M. Rogers.

Rogers remembered that she had worried about injuring Elisabeth by pressing her too vigorously to walk, but a surgeon who knew Elisabeth well told her, "Don't worry, she's as tough as a pine knot." Rogers said Elisabeth loved the phrase and that she asked her to call her "pine knot" afterward.

At 1:30 a.m. on December 14, 1950, just eleven days before her 83rd birthday, Elisabeth died at her home at 614 Park Avenue. Her sister, Alice, had died five years earlier.

Elisabeth's last words, according to Anne Rogers, were the first names of her household servants of many years: Irene Whittington and Lillie Mae Everett.

The Baltimore papers printed long obituaries, as did the *New York Times*. In each obituary she was identified, if not in the first paragraph of the article (as in the *Times*), but in the second or third paragraph, as the "daughter of Daniel Coit Gilman, first president of Johns Hopkins University."

She had adored her father. But after all the years that had passed since his death and after all she had accomplished on her own, one wonders if she would have been happier simply to have been remembered as "Elisabeth Gilman, Socialist and civil rights leader."

At a testimonial dinner in her honor nine years earlier, her Episcopal clergyman, Reverend Arthur B. Kinsolving, of Old St. Paul's Church, said, "I have never met anybody with a more direct intuitional faculty for discovering a need. She inherited her genius in this respect from her father. The daughter is equal to the father."

He added, "She is one of the truest Christians I have known in a ministry of nearly sixty years."

On Friday, December 15, the day before her funeral service, the *Evening Sun* remembered her on the editorial page under a simple headline, "Miss Gilman." The editorial noted she was "in the familiar phrase, a character, but the expression was used of her with great respect, for it was generally acknowledged that she was a woman of great character."

During her lifetime, the editor wrote, she frequently was

> a storm center—but the storms which revolved about her, or rather her ideas and her causes, were not disturbing and ill-tempered and exhausting but rather lively and good natured and often invigorating. That was Miss Gilman's great contribution to Baltimore as a citizen.

Her funeral, on Saturday, December 16, 1950, was held at Old St. Paul's Church where the seeds of her faith had been planted so many years before.

Close friends gathered early that morning at 614 Park Avenue for a brief memorial service. Then they made their way to Old St. Paul's in time for the 10 a.m. service, which was led by the Rector, Harry Lee Doll. Following the service, they gathered again at the well-known Druid Ridge Cemetery at 7900 Park Heights Avenue in the Pikesville section of Baltimore, where Elisabeth was laid to rest.

Nowhere among her papers is there any indication why she chose to be buried in a Baltimore County cemetery rather than in the family plot in Norwich, Connecticut, where her father, mother, and stepmother were buried. But one might assume that by the time she selected her gravesite she knew that she wanted to lie in the community and state to which she had become so attached.

Only a few days after her funeral and burial, the *Evening Sun* reported that her Will had been filed in Orphans' Court. She had left the largest part of her estate to the Christian Social Justice Fund, an organization about which little seemed to be known in Baltimore.

Elisabeth and Mercer Johnston had created the Fund many years earlier to support liberal and religious organizations. Johnston was the first president of the CSJF and Elisabeth was secretary for many years. A group of like-minded friends comprised the board of trustees that oversaw disbursements. Elisabeth often made personal contributions to the Fund.

The executors and trustees of her estate were James B. Diggs and S. Page Nelson, the same Page Nelson who had lived with Elisabeth during his student days at Johns Hopkins and, at her death, was the treasurer of the university.

It is strange that neither Diggs nor Nelson said they knew much about the Christian Social Justice Fund. *The Evening Sun* reported that they were unable "to give a precise description of the ... Fund's functions. Both said, however, it was a charity organization rather than a political action fund."

One suspects they knew a lot about the Fund but simply did not want to comment on it in the press.

Elisabeth left the bulk of the residue of her estate to support a fund to promote socialism. She named Norman Thomas and the Socialist leader Harry W. Ladler as the two persons she wanted to administer the fund. She also left each of them $100.

She gave nothing to Johns Hopkins University, saying she had made generous gifts to the university during her lifetime. She left a small portion of the residue to Gilman School.

Mercer Johnston, with whom Elisabeth had served in France and in the Open Forum, and his wife, Katherine, each received a $500 annuity. Elisabeth also left Katherine a solitaire diamond brooch.

Mercer and Katherine did not attend Elisabeth's funeral. Among his papers is a small envelope containing a card that had been printed before Elisabeth's death. Blank spaces had been left for the date and time of her death and the date, time, and place of her funeral. The spaces had been filled in by hand and the card was sent to the Johnstons and, presumably, many others. Mercer had scrawled across the envelope, in a soft pencil, "Arrived too late." A sad ending to a long, and, at times, intense, association.

If Mercer ever wrote a letter of thanks or appreciation for his friend and patron, to her or to the lawyers who settled her estate, none was to be found.

Through her bequest, Elisabeth continued to assist Mercer and Katherine for the remainder of their lives. And yet Mercer still was unable to express a word of appreciation for her extraordinary generosity and friendship over a period of more than 40 years.

Fortunately, there were countless others who did speak up to express the profoundly positive impact that Elisabeth had during her eight decades on earth. The *Evening Sun* editors may have summed it up best when they wrote in an editorial:

> She had the ability to prod people—usually agreeably—into thinking and rethinking, even when they concluded that her position on whatever cause she was currently espousing, was a mistaken one.

They concluded:

> Yet she was not by any means simply a contentious and 'argufying' woman. Indeed, the very reverse is true as the affectionate references to her as 'Miss Lizzie" indicate. Even those who took issue with her most strongly will realize that Baltimore has lost a personality and link with the calmer and more spacious past.

AFTERWORD

Many of the social reforms Elisabeth Gilman fought for over a period of nearly four decades had not been completed at the time of her death and many she wrestled with are still with us today.

Consider a few: poverty, civil rights, racial discrimination, women's rights, social justice, high-quality public education, fair wages, decent working conditions, broad access to reasonable housing and aid for the homeless, financial security for the elderly, widely available public transportation, and fair and generous immigration policies.

Had she lived in the era of debates about making more and better health care available to our citizens, here is little doubt that she would have been a staunch ally for those who urge the development of a system of accessible, fairly-priced care for everyone.

Social reforms today most often are advocated by large groups of individuals gathered under the banners of organizations focused on a single subject: health, justice, environment, civil rights, education, and the like.

Today one is hard pressed to imagine the presence of a single individual, like Elisabeth Gilman, who could draw so much public attention to the need for reform, justice, and equity in so many areas of our society. That she did so with extraordinary energy, commitment, and grace earned her well-deserved accolades throughout her life.

The public may have seen Elisabeth as a no-nonsense, old-fashioned Victorian woman always battling for solutions to social issues she promoted. But there also was another Elisabeth, a woman living out the tenets of her religious beliefs, and at the same time, discovering that she had become vulnerable, late in life, to an emotional relationship with a man for whom she had profound admiration and affection.

Her papers and those of Mercer Green Johnston reached out to me with a fascinating story that deserved to be told, and it was my privilege to do so.

ACKNOWLEDGMENTS

T he following persons were extremely helpful to me at critical periods throughout the several years I spent researching and writing the manuscript for this book.

Special Collections, Sheridan Libraries, The Johns Hopkins University
- James Stimpert, Senior Reference Archivist
- Amy Kimball, Head, Materials Management
- Heidi Herr, Outreach Librarian

Evergreen Museum and Library of The Johns Hopkins University
- James A. Abbott, Philip F. Wagley Director and Curator
- Nancy Powers, Museum Services Coordinator
- Ben Renwick, Facilities and Operations Coordinator

Through their generosity I was able to spend quiet, uninterrupted time at Evergreen preparing the manuscript.

Nancy McCall, director of the Alan Mason Chesney Medical Archives of the Johns Hopkins Medical Institutions, led me to correspondence I might not have found without her assistance.

Mary Kline, Archivist of the Episcopal Diocese of Maryland,

opened relevant files which helped me gain a greater understanding of social outreach programs of the church to which Elisabeth was so faithful.

Eric Stoykovich, Historical Manuscripts Project Archivist, Special Collections, University of Maryland, helped me obtain photographs of Elisabeth Gilman.

Ryan Bean at the Kautz Family YMCA Archives, University of Minnesota, enabled me to find some specific information about Mercer Johnston's YMCA service in France in World War I.

The archivists at the Library of Congress, Washington, D.C., were generous with their time and helpful and responsive to my questions related to the papers of Mercer Green Johnston.

I found only two persons who had met and spent time with Elisabeth. They were Page Nelson and his sister, Julie Nelson Williams. I interviewed Page Nelson at his home in Centreville, Delaware, and spoke by phone with his sister, Julia Nelson Williams, from her home in Williamsburg, Virginia. Their father, Page, was one of the many students who lived in Elisabeth's home at 513 Park Avenue, Baltimore, over a period of many years. Page and Julia remembered that, as children, they accompanied their parents on frequent visits to Elisabeth's home for Sunday dinners. Their recollections of those visits helped me gain a better understanding of the elegant Victorian setting in which Elisabeth lived.

Susan DePasquale: I express my deepest appreciation to this highly talented and experienced writer and editor who not only edited my initial drafts but wrote several articles about Miss Lizzie and my efforts to produce a book about her. Sue was always available for advice and consultation. No matter what the issue may have been, she addressed it with optimism, good cheer, and encouragement.

Ronald Sauder generously agreed to bring this book to the

public through his Secant Publishing company. For that and for his friendship over many years I shall be forever grateful.

Maria Nealon Jones, my daughter-in-law, helped on many occasions to wrestle information from my laptop and put the manuscript in good order. My gratitude overflows.

Finally, to Lynn, my dear wife and closest companion for more than six decades, I express unbounded appreciation. She encouraged me when I said I wanted to write about Elisabeth's life, listened patiently when I enthused about details I discovered during my research, and never complained when the project took much longer to complete than either of us had anticipated.

APPENDIX: A QUIET DAY, 513 PARK AVENUE

Among Elisabeth's papers is an interesting, amusing account of a guest's visit to her home at 513 Park Avenue, Baltimore, and their Sunday afternoon jaunt to the Baltimore City Jail.

It apparently was written by a friend, a woman, presumably, but there is no indication of when it was written, who the woman was, where she came from, or how long she stayed.

(It is unlikely that she was from Baltimore, since, in her account of the day, she mistook Fort McHenry, which Baltimoreans know is in their city, for Fort Sumter, in Charleston, South Carolina.)

Whatever the case, Elisabeth saved her guest's recollections. Perhaps she enjoyed her friend's style and humor, or maybe she appreciated the description of herself as a highly energized, indefatigable woman, who was always ready to lend a helping hand to people far beneath her on the city's social ladder. Perhaps her friend sent it to her some years afterward as a reminder—a souvenir—of a whirlwind day that both of them had enjoyed.

Because it is humorous and because it provides an intimate snapshot of one afternoon with Elisabeth, it seemed useful to include it in its entirety (complete with eccentricities of punctuation and spelling).

A Quiet Day, 513 Park Avenue

I shall never forget, as long as I live, the Day after Christmas that I spent with Elisabeth Gilman. (Yes—of course. But let me tell about My Day with her!)

Her sister, Mrs. Wheeler, had come from New York, to spend the holidays with Elisabeth. Warily, to be sure; and mostly in her room; safe from the Chinese, Spanish, and ordinary incendiaries, apt to be found downstairs. But she was there; and E.G. invited me to come meet her; if not on Christmas, then on the day after; which, this year, fell upon the Sabbath.

One might pardonably suppose that Sunday, which Elisabeth starts with church – and that, the most respectable in Baltimore, under dear old Dr. Kinsolving; whose actions are planted in Trinity Church, Boston, and in John Nicholas Brown's family in Newport … one might safely think that Sunday, so begun, would be a pale day – reserved; and proud.

I arrived just at noon. Sure enough, there was Mrs. Wheeler, at dinner. The placid meal, decked with eight generations of silver, and hovered over by James, whose many years of tender care both of the aristocracy and the wayfaring man have given him an aplomb and a technique perfectly unequalled – the meal, passed from sherry to icecream without a pause. I forget how many were there; I think fourteen. But as this was not a Forum Sunday, the company was notable merely for its charm. Mrs. Wheeler breathed freely; and although she retreated to her room after coffee, there was really no immediate reason for her to do so. For E.G. and I, and I may say, the Dogs, were only going to the Penitentiary. The house would be perfectly calm.

It seemed that Elisabeth had had a letter from a friend, who was serving two years for mayhem; and, not unnaturally, he wanted her to get him out. With the letter came two Gifts, One was a large cross, made from carefully jig-sawed pieces of wood, varnished glitteringly with orange; the second was a picture frame, of the same color and craftsmanship, complete with a picture of Clark Gable.

The donor wrote that he had sat on a platform with E.G. at a labor meeting years before and had been friends with her ever since.

Well, one word to E.G. is enough. Dogs in hand—or, rather, she and I attached to leashes behind Slivers and YoHo, whose blue blood has not sapped their vitality, set out, headlong, to the jail. E.G. is small but dauntless; but even she was more or less breathless, and I was totally undone, after running, thirty miles an hour, through the streets of Baltimore.

In the vestibule of the prison, two little colored boys offered to hold the leashes; and the dogs, who share their Mistress's adaptability to all sorts and conditions of men, amiably and immediately took charge of the boys while we stepped inside.

The wardens, sheriffs, and whoever the other guardians were who were lounging in the ante-room, leaped to their feet when they saw who we were. Doors swung before us, and going down some stairs, we were shortly in the visitors' room; with the Friend across the table from us.

What a Friend! He had lost one ear, as a sailor; his nose was permanently bashed in and his head had a remarkable likeness to a cannon ball. Leaning eagerly across the table, where he was allowed to talk freely, he began. Now unfortunately, E.G. sometimes misses a word, and as fifty other friends were shouting to their visitors around us, she poked me to translate. My idealism is not as firm as hers; so that I was quite shocked.

'Listen, said the Friend. 'Listen. I KNOW this Lady, see? Now, if she'll slip the Governor $500.00, (that's the way things work, see?) I'd get out in about six weeks, see? You needn't even SAY it's for me—he could use five hundred, see, for a new car, see, any time. Just GET it to him! And ask I should get out, see? So I didn't do nuttin'. They was a fight and they pinned it on me when Joe got knocked out. He only got a broken skull, see. You tell her. It'll only be $500.00!'

Speechless with the impossibility of conveying in a loud voice with all the guards around us and already in the jail, to E.G., what her Friend's message was; and speechless to interpret to him, her anxiety to know if he really had bitten the ear of his seaside opponent, or if the charge were false—I could only wave my hands and say "No, No!" to them both. This interchange, if such it could be called – E.G. leaning eagerly forward – he pommelling the table – I feebly waving my hands, continued; until, to the relief of all concerned, the Guard removed the Friend. I waited, until we got up and out, to explain the mystery to Elisabeth.

She did not turn a hair. "Well, I can't give him $5,00.00. But I will write today to the Pardon Board – for I don't believe he did it! "

This sublime faith, after confronting his absent ear and nose, I could not match… We untangled the Dogs from the [boys], and proceeded, as thoughtfully as possible, toward 513. (I don't think it was that same day that she took me to see Fort Sumter – or is it Fort Sumter? The Fort in the extreme tip of Baltimore, where they first sang the Star Spangled Banner – E.G. adores forts; and this, as the Walrus said, is very queer, because she is a Pacifist- a Militant one.)

It was fortunate that we were taken by the Dogs to tea, on the way home; for in the course of natural events, in the hour after we came in, the house filled up with:

- A White Russian ex-Prince, who had married a Baltimorean.
- A Jewish Friend of the Soviets.
- A former professor, who had undertaken to help the Share Croppers; who wanted to tell E.G. that Sherwood Eddy was a Snake.

- A colored lady, member of the Socialist Party, to plan for a committee meeting.
- I think there was a Chinese, but I got a little blurred at this point.
- Another Socialist, to report on Help for the Spanish Republic.

P.S. They all stayed for supper. And we went to a Socialist meeting in the Evening – Mrs. Wheeler, I did not see, again.

BIBLIOGRAPHY

Nearly all of the sources I used to write this account of Elisabeth Gilman's life are contained in three main categories:

(1) Her personal papers containing letters, diaries, a brief memoir, scrapbooks, and newspaper clippings. They are located in the Ferdinand Hamburger Archives at Johns Hopkins University.
(2) Newspaper accounts of her many activities spanning more than sixty years.
(3) Correspondence between Elisabeth and Mercer Green Johnston in a collection at the Library of Congress labeled Mercer Green Johnston Papers 1860-1954.

The Hamburger Archives also provided relevant material in the papers of Elizabeth Dwight Woolsey Gilman (Elisabeth's stepmother) and in The Daniel Coit Gilman Papers (1873-1942). Other materials that proved helpful were in the collections of the Alan Mason Chesney Medical Archives of the Johns Hopkins Medical Institutions.

Materials in the Archives of the Episcopal Diocese of Maryland were helpful. The Kautz Family YMCA Archives at the University of Minnesota provided information about Mercer Johnston's service in World War I.

Newspaper accounts of Elisabeth's social activism and political campaigning were invaluable in tracing her lifetime of service to others. I found accounts about her in the following newspapers: *The Baltimore Sun, The Baltimore Evening Sun, The Baltimore News, The Baltimore American, The Baltimore Afro-American, The Baltimore Leader, The Maryland Leader, The Hagerstown* (Maryland) *Morning Herald, The Frederick News*, and *The New York Times*.

In a time when so much well-sourced information is available online, I made use of such information through numerous websites.

Three manuscripts shed light on Elisabeth's affiliation with the Episcopal Church and Rev. Mercer Green Johnston.

- "An Account of My Stewardship: Mercer Green Johnston, the Episcopal Church and the Social Gospel in Newark, NJ, 1912-1916," by Jeremy Bonner, an online research article in Anglican and Episcopal history, published by Questia.
- "The Anglican, Episcopal and Diocesan Heritage in Maryland," an unpublished manuscript in the Episcopal Diocese of Maryland Archives, by D. Randall Beirne.
- "A History of the First 100 Years of the Boy's School of St. Paul's Parish." The Rev. Arthur B. Kinsolving. Accessed at the Episcopal Diocese of Maryland.

The following books were helpful:

- *A History of the University Founded by Johns Hopkins*. John C. French, Johns Hopkins University Press, 1946.
- *Pioneer: A History of The Johns Hopkins University 1974-1889*. Hugh Hawkins, Cornell University Press, 1960.
- *Daniel C. Gilman: Creator of the American Type of University*. Abraham Flexner, Harcourt Brace & Co., 1946.

Information contained in these books provided insights into particular aspects of Elisabeth's life:

- *The Business of Travel: Place, Faith and History*. Philip Scranton and Janet F. Davidson, editors. University of Pennsylvania Press, 2007.
- *Daily Life During World War I*. Neil M. Heyman, The Greenwood Press (Daily Life Through History Series), 2002.
- *In Uncle Sam's Service: Women Workers with the AEF 1917-1919*. Susan Zeiger, University of Pennsylvania Press, 2004.
- *Kingdom to Commune: Protestant Pacifist Culture Between World War I and the Viet Nam Era*. Patricia Appelbaum, University of North Carolina Press, 2009.

ABOUT THE AUTHOR

Ross Jones retired as Vice President and Secretary of Johns Hopkins University in 2003, after more than four decades in the administration. He was a close associate of six of the university's presidents and five chairmen of the Board of Trustees. An alumnus of Johns Hopkins, he went on to earn a graduate degree in journalism from Columbia University. He worked briefly as a reporter on newspapers in Pennsylvania and New York before returning to his alma mater. He served three years in the U.S. Army.

INDEX

S

"Saul" (Browning), 74
Save Our Schools (SOS) Committee, 117
school conditions, 64
Scudder, Vida Dutton, 79–80, 123, 186, 197
seasickness, 53–54
Seger, Gerhart, 203
Settlement Houses, 79
Shaw, Tom, 111
Sheffield Scientific School (at Yale), 5, 17
Sherwood Forest conference, 80–83, 84–87, 143
Sigerist, Henry E., 199
Sinclair, Upton, 82, 163
Smiley, J.F., 161
Smith, Al, 184
Soboloff, Simon, 233
Social Democratic League of America, 132
Social Gospel movement
    about, 59, 69
    Gilman, E., work on, 85–86, 186
    and Johnston, M., 83, 87, 129, 134
    and Rauschenbusch, 84
    and Scudder, 79–80
Social Security, 116
social workers, origins of, 62
Socialism. *See also* Sherwood Forest conference; Social Gospel Movement
    and the church, 69, 74, 79–80
    vs communism, 169
    decline of, 183–187
    in Europe, 166–167
    Gilman, E., political campaigns of (*See* Gilman, Elisabeth (Lizzie): political campaigns)
    and the Great Depression, 185–186
    Johnston, M. on, 121
    media, 143, 173–174, 184
    and patriotism, 86
    presidential campaign, 1928, 159
    and the Progressive Party, 183
    in Russia, 166–167
    and violence, 185
    on World War I, 184–185
"Socialist Looks at The Rapid Transit Situation, A" (Gilman, E.), 211
Socialist Party. *See* Socialism
Society of Nations, The (Morley), 167
Spanish Civil War, 198–200
Spargo, John, 84
Springside School, 26
St. Paul's Episcopal Church, 69–70
Starr, Ellen Gates, 60
Stern, Hugo, 167
Stokes, James Graham Phelps, 85, 122
Stokes, Rose Pastor, 122
strike reliefs, 113–116, 148, 180–182, 189, 212
students, college, 82
suffrage, 122, 124, 135. *See also* women
Summer, Helen L., 82
Sun, The (Baltimore newspaper). *See* newspaper mentions
Sunday Sun, 195. *See also* newspaper mentions

T

Taylor, Clarence, 168
Teacher's Oath Bill, 202–203
Thomas, Norman
    about, 159, 167–168
    and Gilman, E. estate, 239
    as presidential candidate, 184, 186, 191
    at testimonial dinner for Gilman, E., 233–235
    and unemployment, 188
Thomas Cook & Son (travel company), 44–45
Toole, William A., 161, 214
Toynbee Hall, 60–61
transportation systems, 211
travel, of the wealthy, 44–45. *See also* Gilman, Elisabeth (Lizzie): travels of

U
Ulman, Joseph, 233
unemployment, 63, 76, 168, 188–189, 190
unions, labor, 111–112
United Railways, 211
University of California, 12–14

V
Van Antwerp, John, 167
Van Nuys, Frederick, 197
Verdun (France), 108, 109
Villard, Oswald Garrison, 118, 154–156, 220
Voice of the People, The, 133–134, 136, 141

W
Wagner, Robert F., 197
Waldman, Louis, 167–168
Warbass, James P., 82
Ward, Nathaniel, 58
Wardell, Miss, 23–24
Washington, George, 17, 55
Watson, James B., 27–28
Webb, Mrs. Sidney, 167
wedding, of Gilman, D. and Gilman, E. (Lilly), 20–21
Weinstein, James, 184
Welch, William H., 164, 174, 229
welfare agencies, during World War I, 89
Wellesley College, 79
Wheeler, Alice (sister)
  and 614 Park Avenue, 220–221
  death of, 236
  and father relationship, 5, 29
  Gilman, M. on, 6
  husband of, 134–135
  and sister relationship, 67
  travels with
    Egypt, 1890, 43–49
    Europe, 1889, 36–39, 41
    Europe, 1900, 53–57
    Greek Islands and Turkey, 1890, 51–52

    Holy Lands, 1890, 49–51
    Nile River, 1890, 44–49
    Northern Africa, 1889-1890, 39–42
Wheeler, Benjamin Ide, 55
Wheeler, Burton K., 113, 146, 158
Wheeler, Everett P. (brother-in-law), 134–135, 222
Wheeler Defense Fund, 146
White, Andrew, 8, 14, 15, 34, 73
White, William Allen, 118
Whitfield, Stephen J., 122
Whitmore, Clarence, 168
Whittington, Irene, 236
Willard, Mary Hatch, 93–94
Williams, Charles D., 138
Williams, Matthew, 198
Wilmer, William H., 174
women
  Afro-American votes, 172
  and social and political issues, 122, 124, 135
  trade issues, 111, 191
  in World War I, 89–92, 96–98
Women's Club of Baltimore, 67
Women's Division of the LaFollette-Wheeler Presidential campaign, 113
Women's Trade Union League of America, The, 111
Woolley, Mary, 118
Woolsey, Elizabeth Dwight. *See* Gilman, Elizabeth Dwight (Lilly; stepmother)
Woolsey, John, 21
Woolsey, Theodore Dwight, 20
Worker's Defense League (WDL), 203–204
World War I
  and air raid, 100–101
  canteens in, 88, 90–91, 97
  Christmas during, 98–99
  end of, 106–108

Gilman, E. in (*See* Gilman, Elisabeth
(Lizzie): in World War I)
Gilman, E. on, 96–97, 192–195
social issues, post, 85
Socialists on, 184–185
women in, 88–92, 96–98

Y
Yale University, 5, 9, 17
YMCA (Young Men's Christian Associa-
tion), 87–92, 95, 97, 104, 193
Young Pioneers of America, The,
116–117